# What will it take to end child poverty?

**Available in alternative formats**

This publication can be provided in alternative formats such as large print, Braille, audiotape and on disk. Please contact: Communications Department, Joseph Rowntree Foundation, The Homestead, 40 Water End, York YO30 6WP. Tel: 01904 615905. Email: info@jrf.org.uk

# What will it take to end child poverty?
## Firing on all cylinders

Donald Hirsch

JOSEPH ROWNTREE
FOUNDATION

The **Joseph Rowntree Foundation** has supported this project as part of its programme of research and innovative development projects, which it hopes will be of value to policy makers, practitioners and service users. The facts presented and views expressed in this report are, however, those of the author and not necessarily those of the Foundation.

Joseph Rowntree Foundation
The Homestead
40 Water End
York YO30 6WP
**Website:** www.jrf.org.uk

ISBN-13:   978 1 85935 499 5
ISBN-10:   1 85935 499 8

A pdf version of this publication is available from the JRF website (www.jrf.org.uk).

A CIP catalogue record for this report is available from the British Library.

Designed by Adkins Design
Printed by Fretwells Ltd.

Further copies of this report, or any other JRF publication, can be obtained either from the JRF website (www.jrf.org.uk/bookshop/) or from our distributor, York Publishing Services (Tel: 01904 430033).

# Contents

# Acknowledgements

This project was a collaborative venture that drew on contributions and advice from a range of experts. Jonathan Bradshaw, James Browne, Mike Brewer, Nick Gould, Paul Gregg, Susan Harkness, Stephen Machin, Lindsey Macmillan, Sandra McNally, John Parsons, Phil Rees and Holly Sutherland all contributed to working papers on which this report draws (see list in Appendix).

In addition, Stephen Alambritis, Paul Dornan, Richard Exell, Goretti Horgan, Peter Kelly, Mike Lewis, Colette Marshall, Laura Payne, Stephen Meek, Bob Reitemeier, Elaine Squires and Madeleine Tearse gave advice and support to the project as members of the advisory group and in many other ways.

Sue Middleton contributed both by helping conceptualise the project at its start and by commenting on drafts towards its completion.

Helen Barnard and Chris Goulden at JRF held all this together and therefore made it possible for a highly ambitious project to bear fruit.

I am grateful to all of these people, and to the many who contributed in regional feedback events, for the time and effort devoted to this worthwhile enterprise.

# Introduction
## The purpose of this report

In 1999 Tony Blair announced the historic aim of ending child poverty within a generation. In 2006, Conservative policy director Oliver Letwin announced that his party shares that ambition. While poverty has many dimensions and many definitions, this shared mission has given our society and our government a core set of targets which, if fulfilled, will go a long way towards ending the worst forms of hardship suffered today by millions of children growing up in families with low incomes.

The central objective of ensuring that children do not have to live in households with incomes below a certain level, relative to contemporary norms, has produced some specific target milestones. These are that the percentage of children in households with below 60 per cent median income should fall from its 1998/99 level by a quarter by 2004/05, by half by 2010 and to a minimal level (variously interpreted as between 5 per cent and 10 per cent of children) by 2020.

In 2006, data on the first target showed that a substantial fall in child poverty had gone most, but not all, of the way towards meeting it. While this may be taken to show that the government is 'nearly on target' in carrying forward its long-term anti-poverty drive, the situation is in fact more complicated. This is because measures that succeed in raising the first quarter of children out of poverty, if simply carried forward, will be less effective in reducing poverty among the other three quarters, whose situation is more severe.

The Joseph Rowntree Foundation has brought together leading experts in this field to consider what needs to happen now in order to maintain the required progress (see the Appendix for details of this project). This report sets out their findings. It starts by looking at the nature and underlying causes of the problem of child poverty in the UK, and then considers the various factors that can contribute to its eradication. Chapter 4 reports specifically on a modelling exercise that projects the effect of current policies on future levels of child poverty and looks at what new policies might be capable of in terms of meeting or progressing towards the 2010 and 2020 targets.

This exercise needs to be understood in the context of what it is trying to do and what it is not.

First, the focus of this report is on meeting relative income targets. The fall in the percentage of children on relatively low incomes is an important but not the only indicator of reduced hardship among poor children. One other indicator being adopted by the government, which measures material deprivation, will also be valuable, but is not yet adequately developed to be subject to these projections. More generally, overall government progress in tackling childhood disadvantage will be judged by a wider range of criteria than those on which this report concentrates, including the extent of experiences such as homelessness and other forms of disadvantage.

Second, while the report refers to a wide range of factors that will influence relative incomes, it is not able to project the long-term impact of all these influences. When thinking about child poverty in 2020, we are considering children who have not yet been born, many of whose parents are themselves still young children today. Ambitious policies to eradicate child poverty need to influence their futures and opportunities through changes in society that cannot be projected in the same way as more direct measures, such as moving individuals into work or increasing tax credits. Our modelling work concentrates on the latter.

For these reasons, this report is not a blueprint for a full programme to end child poverty. Nevertheless, its findings are immensely important for the design of long-term strategies. The results give an indication of the magnitude of the task ahead and of the extra measures, with both tangible and less measurable impacts, that will need to be introduced in order to fulfil it.

# Executive summary

In the past two decades of the 20th century, children replaced old people as the group most likely to be in poverty in the UK. The proportion living in families with low incomes doubled. The present government has the bold ambition of halving child poverty again by 2010, and of ending it by 2020. It has made a start, with the child poverty rate now falling steadily, even though by less than was needed to meet the interim targets of a one quarter reduction by 2004. This report looks at what needs to happen for the fall to continue and to accelerate, in order to get back on track.

## Child poverty: a damaging, avoidable feature of modern Britain

Poverty in this report is measured in terms of relative income: children living in households with below 60 per cent of the median are defined as poor. However, poverty in the UK is more than just a statistical artefact. Millions of children are unable to enjoy the basic living standards that their peers take for granted. Some lack physical basics like adequate clothing and a balanced diet. Many others are unable to participate fully in society, for example because their parents cannot afford to pay for activities outside the home, and they do not feel they can invite friends round for tea or a snack.

Child poverty is not a uniform phenomenon: the one in four children on relatively low incomes have a range of life experiences. Some are temporarily in poverty, others have to suffer it for years. For most, it is not transitionary: two thirds of poor children have been poor in at least three of the past four years. Some children face deep poverty, and certain groups are particularly vulnerable to severe hardship, including homeless children, those with disabled parents and children of marginalised groups including asylum seekers and Travellers. Child poverty is also influenced by where you live. Within Great Britain, London and North East England have the highest poverty rates, but the real concentrations come at the more local level. The majority of children in some wards grow up poor.

Nor does child poverty damage only those it affects directly: it makes all of society poorer. This is true not only in moral terms, but also literally. Child poverty brings a wide range of tangible costs, ranging from paying for services required as a result of the fall-out of children growing up poor, to foregone taxes and higher benefits resulting from reduced future employment prospects of those who experience childhood poverty. The financial cost of ending child poverty in a generation needs to be set against the cost for many generations to come of not ending it. The intergenerational 'knock-on' effect of children growing up poor, and then becoming poor parents themselves, appears to be escalating. The negative effect on prospects in adulthood of experiencing childhood poverty has grown from one cohort to the next.

High levels of child poverty as seen in the UK are neither inevitable nor shared by most similar countries. Even after the most recent UK fall, only Italy, Portugal and the Slovak Republic have higher rates among the 25 European Union (EU) countries. Contributory factors have included pay inequalities, a high proportion of lone parents, their low chance of working and less generous government redistribution than most other countries. The last two of these have started to change, but there remains a long way to go.

## Implementing a wide-ranging strategy

Ending child poverty is only partly about transferring money to poor households. A long-term solution must involve much more, tackling the root causes of poverty and in particular giving families opportunities that help them gain greater control of their own lives. Government initiatives have started to make progress in this direction, but there remain large unfinished agendas.

One key priority of the current Labour government is to help more parents on low incomes to move into work. The direct way of doing so is through New Deal programmes that give assistance in finding jobs. Such programmes have contributed to a big expansion in employment, and a reduction by a quarter in the number of workless households. However, as time goes on, those who remain out of work become harder to help, because they are people facing greater barriers to employment. For example, half of children with parents claiming out-of-work benefits now either have a parent who is disabled, or are under five and have a lone parent. In this context, measures to promote employment must do much more than help people find work: in some cases giving individuals intensive support and advice, and in others addressing barriers to working such as the lack of adequate childcare. Despite a range of initiatives to improve childcare, many parents still find it impossible to make satisfactory arrangements.

In future, it would be unwise to rely too much on movement from welfare to work as a means of reducing poverty. In recent years it has made a contribution, but a diminishing one, accounting for only about a sixth of the reduction in child poverty between 1998-99 and 2004-05. Even if the government meets its targets to raise employment rates, especially among lone parents, this will go only a small way to achieving the targets for reducing child poverty. Moreover, a strategy that relied excessively on getting as many parents as possible into jobs may prioritise this at the expense of family life. Parents want to be able to find their own balance between looking after their children and providing for them economically, and not be told that work must always come first.

One requirement in promoting this choice is that having no worker in the family should not, as at present, make it far more likely than not that a child will face poverty. The introduction of the Child Tax Credit has helped improve the relative incomes of families outside work as well as in it, but there remains a long way to go. Even though present policy guarantees that the part of this credit targeted at lower-income families will rise in line with earnings, current uprating policies overall are not sufficient to keep out-of-work incomes in line with living standards, let alone enable them to rise so that relative poverty falls.

At the same time, the experiences of people in work can be as important as whether or not they can find jobs. Better pay, secure employment, improved work–life balance and in some cases the chance to increase the number of working hours in a household can all help improve families' life chances, and give them more control over their lives. Government can contribute to these improvements, partly by working with employers to improve pay, training and conditions at the lower end of the labour market.

But just as important in the long term is to improve education, which can enhance the life chances of tomorrow's parents. One big unfinished agenda for tackling child poverty over the long term is the improvement in educational outcomes for children from disadvantaged families. Educational outcomes in the UK remain more strongly associated with social background than in most other countries, and changing this is a vital part of ending the intergenerational cycle of child poverty.

## Modelling the future: what is needed to hit the targets

As part of this project, microsimulation modelling was used to project the future level of child poverty, under current and alternative policies. Such modelling can only take account of some factors, and therefore cannot be used to design a complete strategy to bring the rate of child poverty down. But it gives an idea of the size of the contribution that some key policies could make to meeting the 2010 and 2020 targets.

The model looked first at what current tax credit, benefit and welfare to work policies are likely to mean for child poverty, in combination with known changes in the characteristics of the population. Some of these characteristics, such as a better-educated group of lone parents, will have a benign effect on child poverty. Nevertheless, with present policies there will be little net change from the present level. The effect of rising employment is likely to be small, while planned rises in some tax credits will be counteracted by falls in relative terms in others and in some benefits. Therefore, without new policies that have substantial effects, the steady fall in child poverty since the 1990s could soon stall.

In order to succeed in halving child poverty by 2010, the most cost-effective single policy measure would be to raise the part of Child Tax Credit targeted on poor families by nearly 50 per cent in real terms. To achieve the same by raising Child Benefit would be three times as expensive. However, a more balanced policy package would use a combination of raising Child Tax Credit with other measures targeted at groups with high poverty risk. One such group is large families, and increases for such families in Child Benefit or in the portion of Child Tax Credit that goes to all but the best-off families would be relatively cost-efficient. Another potential part of the package is a rise in Working Tax Credit for couples, who at present get less favourable treatment with this credit than lone parents.

The total cost of a policy package that achieves the 2010 target is around £4-5 billion. This is a large amount in absolute terms, but represents only about 0.3 per cent of gross domestic product (GDP), and nearly two thirds of it would need to be spent anyway for the country to maintain the present share of national income devoted to supporting the income of families with children.

The cost of meeting the 2020 targets of ending child poverty, mainly using tax and benefits policy, is much higher. Even though the objective is interpreted as getting measured poverty to very low levels (below 5 per cent) rather than all the way to zero, it is almost impossible to do this just by increasing benefits and tax credits specifically for children. Only if parent-targeted income, and in particular Income Support for parents, is also raised can the required reduction be achieved. This reduction will also depend on improving tax credit take-up, or a substantial amount of child poverty will always remain.

A package that between 2010 and 2020 uprated with earnings all benefits and tax credits for families with children, and raised Working Tax Credit for couples, would cost £12 billion on top of the earlier reforms, and would get child poverty down from 13 per cent to 8.5 per cent. To go further and get poverty below the 5 per cent target would require increases much faster than earnings – a doubling in real terms of key tax credits and benefits – between 2010 and 2020. This would cost £28 billion, with the total cost between now and 2020 of 'ending' child poverty coming to over £30 billion and nearly 2 per cent of GDP. This still amounts to less than one year's economic growth over the next 14 years, but would require substantially higher taxation.

The increases shown in this modelling to meet the 2010 target would be feasible, with strong political commitment; they are significantly less than increases seen earlier in the Labour administration. In this relatively short period, when wider policies may not have time to take full effect, there is a case for relying heavily on a further hike in tax credits and benefits. In the period to 2020, on the other hand, it seems inconceivable that poverty will be wiped out through these direct measures alone: not only is the cost extremely high, but such huge transfers to families with children would look odd compared to other people's entitlements and could distort behaviour. Thus, even though substantial increases will undoubtedly be needed, they will have to be combined with other measures. Only by improving the opportunities of tomorrow's parents to provide for themselves, in particular by improving educational outcomes for today's disadvantaged young people, is there a chance that this bold mission will succeed.

# 1 Eradicating child poverty
## A historic mission

*After child poverty doubled at the end of the last century, tackling it has become a priority ...*

In the past generation, the position of child poverty in the UK has changed in two historically unprecedented ways. The first is that the proportion of children living in relatively poor families has doubled. The second is that a government has stated its intention of eradicating child poverty, within another generation, and started adopting large-scale policies designed to tackle this problem directly.

In the 1980s and early 1990s, the UK became a much more unequal society in terms of income and wealth. In the past decade, despite some progress in the opposite direction, poverty and inequality have remained at high levels. Overall, the percentage of people on relatively low incomes is far higher than in 1979. But the distribution of poverty has also

**Figure 1** In the past generation, children have become the group most at risk of poverty

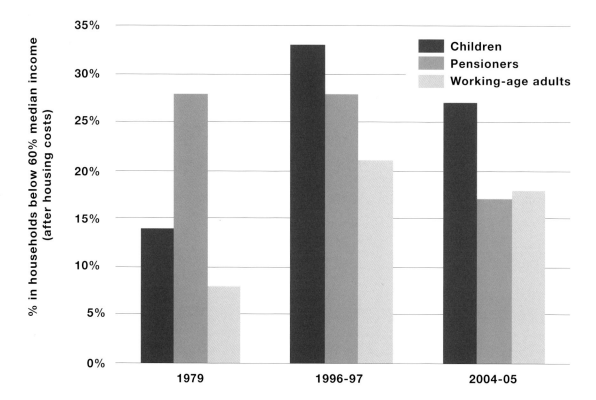

Source: The source of this graph, and of other poverty data in this report where not indicated otherwise, is DWP (2006) *Households below average income 1994/5-2004/5,* London: The Stationery Office. These data cover Britain only, although supplementary data on Northern Ireland are referred to on page 22 below.

changed. In particular, child poverty has grown much faster than poverty overall, and children have replaced pensioners as the demographic group with the highest poverty rates, as shown in Figure 1.

*... with a growing consensus that all children should share in rising living standards.*

While levels of poverty and inequality have not changed much since the mid-1990s, political attitudes towards them have transformed. All political parties have come to accept that relative poverty matters: that as most people in the UK become more prosperous, the country's poorest households should not be left behind. A growing consensus that tackling child poverty should be a special priority has been influenced by several factors. In particular:

- child poverty can cause particular forms of hardship among a group of people who are powerless to change their situation;
- child poverty potentially imposes heavy costs, material and otherwise, on society, today and in years to come;
- international experience shows that the UK level of child poverty is not inevitable.

## Child poverty and the suffering of children

*The need to fight child poverty is rooted in the real hardship that it causes...*

Child poverty has elicited public sympathy, especially in developing countries, because children can be seen as innocent victims. In the UK, where poverty is not killing millions of children a year as elsewhere in the world, the suffering that it does cause is nevertheless clearly not the fault of those who experience it. The evidence shows that this suffering is indeed real. Nearly one in five children surveyed in 1999 lacked at least two things considered by most people in Britain as 'necessities' because their parents could not afford them[1]. About a quarter of a million children had parents who could not afford to buy them a warm coat, about half a million were unable to celebrate special occasions or invite friends round even occasionally for tea or a snack, and over two million did not get even a week's holiday away from home each year because their parents cannot afford it. While these numbers appear to be falling[2], more recent evidence shows that large numbers still lack material necessities (7 per cent of lone parents cannot afford fish or meat every other day) and the ability to interact socially (two in five lone parents and one in ten couple families cannot afford to go on outings or take gifts to parties)[3]. Thus, children who are poor in the UK suffer because they cannot do or cannot have the everyday things that their friends take for granted.

*... and although not every child on low income is deprived ...*

The measure most commonly used to monitor child poverty is the percentage of children at any one time who live below 60 per cent median income (see Box 1). This is an arbitrary

**Box 1: Measuring poverty through relative income**

The most convenient way of continuously monitoring poverty is by looking at the number of people whose incomes fall below a percentage of median income. The median is the income below which exactly half of the population's income falls. In calculating this figure, each individual's *household* income is considered after adjusting for the size and composition of the household. The most common poverty threshold, used across Europe, is 60 per cent of median income.

Income may be considered either before or after housing costs. The latter shows people's disposable income after paying a rent or mortgage, compared to the disposable income of others in the population. This is a useful way of comparing day-to-day living standards, which may not reflect very accurately the amount that people spend on their housing. However, to the extent that being able to afford a higher rent or mortgage is part of reducing poverty and hardship, the before housing cost measure is also of value. This report draws on both measures, but uses the after housing cost measure where not otherwise stated.

**The reality of child poverty: (A) What does it mean in terms of family income?**

What does it mean in financial terms to be poor? In 2004-05, the latest financial year for which income figures are available, poor children were defined as those living in households with incomes below a threshold that varied with family size. For example, a family[4] was defined as poor if it had less than the following amounts each week to pay for everything after covering the rent or mortgage:

**£113** for a lone parent with a 10-month-old baby
**£187** for a lone parent with two children aged 5 and 11
**£269** for a couple with two children aged 5 and 11
**£353** for a couple with four children aged 2, 5, 11 and 14.

(Ready reckoner: start with £183 for a couple or £101 for a lone parent, then add for each child: £13 age 0-1; £33 age 2-4; £38 age 5-7; £42 age 8-10; £48 age 11-12; £51 age 13-15; £70 aged 16-18 and still in full-time education.)

threshold used as an international standard. Although it is very roughly the level needed to purchase goods that have been calculated as necessary for a modern family budget[5], in practice, children below this threshold do not all go without basic necessities, while some children above it are deprived of such items.

*... severe and persistent poverty remain disturbingly high ...*
Yet a 'snapshot' of the number of children below 60 per cent median income tells only part of the story. Among the 3.4 million children classified as being in poor on this measure,

most are in fact considerably poorer, while for the great majority, poverty is not just a transitory experience.

One in six children live in households that are not only below 60 per cent but also below 50 per cent median income. For a lone parent with two children this means getting by on below about £150 a week. As shown in Figure 2, some families are well below even this lower threshold. The risk of this deeper form of poverty is particularly high for non-working families. Half of children with no parent in work fall below this lower threshold. Figure 2 shows a 'bunching' of incomes at around 50 per cent median after housing costs, associated with benefit rates. But not all children with such low family incomes are living on benefits: about a million of those below 50 per cent median have at least one working parent.

## Figure 2 Many children live in families in deep poverty

**Incomes of children below median income, 2004–05**

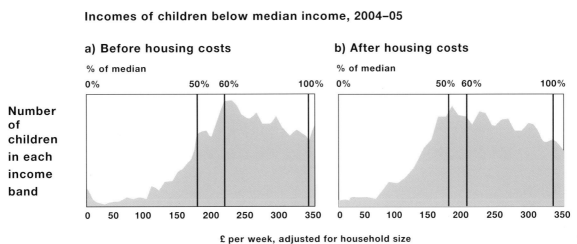

Moreover, while some poor children face only temporary adversity, others remain poor over many years. The continuing degradation of poverty is more likely to scar the childhood of children in persistently poor families, who are unlikely to have spare resources to draw on and more likely to go into debt. Over two thirds of children in households below 60 per cent median income have been in poverty for at least three of the past four years.

Figure 3 shows the substantial numbers in both severe and persistent poverty. Both have been coming down along with overall poverty, when measured after housing costs. Yet with over two million children on less than 50 per cent median income, and a similar number in persistent poverty, after housing costs, there is no room for complacency.

**Figure 3** Behind the headline rates of child poverty, most of the problem remains relatively severe and long-lasting (child poverty rates since 1996–97)

**a) Before housing costs**

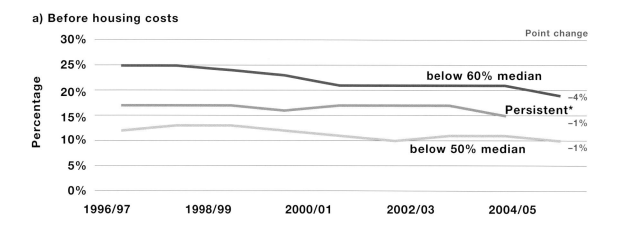

**b) After housing costs**

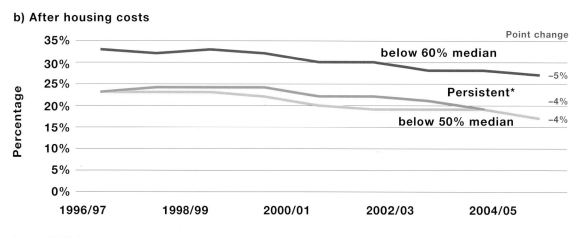

Source: DWP, Households below average income
* Persistent = below 60% median in at least three of past four years

*... while certain groups face particular hardships ...*

At the same time, the experience of poverty can be particularly difficult for certain groups. Among those at greatest risk[6] are:

- **Children in acute housing need.** Over 100,000 children are in homeless families placed in temporary accommodation; around 900,000 are in overcrowded homes; and about half a million are in homes considered unfit for human habitation[7]. (These figures are for England, and overlap.) The hardship of living in housing squalor can dominate the experience of childhood.

- **Children with disabled parents.** One in four children living in poverty has at least one disabled parent. Where such parents do not work, they are less likely to be classified as poor than other workless households, because various disability benefits boost their incomes. However, this classification does not take account of the extra costs of disability, and the extra hardship this may cause. Disabled parents within work, moreover, are more likely than other working parents to remain poor, reflecting difficulties many disabled people have in progressing in the labour market[8]. Thus, children with disabled parents are particularly vulnerable to persistent poverty.

- **Children of asylum seekers,** as well as children who have arrived in the UK without parents, seeking asylum. Children of asylum seekers are excluded from various measures protecting the welfare of other children in the UK. Most fundamentally, they are denied access to even the basic living standards accorded to other children, as their parents only receive Income Support worth 70 per cent of the usual rate, as well as being barred from working while their cases are being considered. Children's charities say that their research shows that this group's status as asylum seekers is given precedence over their status as children[9].

- **Gypsy and Traveller children.** Many of these children face multiple disadvantages, combining financial with other forms of hardship[10]. Participants at a discussion event in Belfast, one of the sessions held by the Joseph Rowntree Foundation seeking feedback on ideas generated by this project, highlighted the particular combination of poverty and prejudice confronting these children. Organisations working with Travellers in other parts of the UK have also identified a wide range of concerns including worse health and education outcomes than settled families.

### Box 2: The reality of child poverty: (B) The lived experience, described by three 12-year-olds

(From *Waiting for the future, Poems by children on poverty and bad housing*, Shelter and End Child Poverty, 2006)

Living in poverty is never wearing something
That someone else has not already worn
Living in poverty is never buying something
That someone else has not already bought
Living in poverty is getting tired of people
Wanting you to be grateful
Living in poverty is checking the coin slot of
Every vending machine as you go by
Living in poverty is hoping your toothache
Will go away
Living in poverty is watching your mum
Making lunch, dropping a piece of meat,
Then looking round to see if anyone saw
Living in poverty is buying a lottery ticket
When you can't afford it
Living in poverty
Still hoping
*Meirion*

He asks for ...
A black leather jacket,
Remote control car,
Nike trainers,
A fancy electric guitar.

A flashy new phone,
A 20gig MP3,
A new mountain bike,
And a flat screen TV.

I ask for ...
A kiss from my mother, a hug from my father,
And a pair of shoes without holes.

Three and a half million of us,
Yet it feels like I'm all alone.
**Helen Monks**

A dark cramped bedroom,
The windows are grey,
Cold porridge for breakfast, Nowhere to play....

I hear my mum crying,
In her bedroom at night.
I go in and tell her
That it's all right....

I wish we had money
Like other kids have,
To buy some clean clothes,
Instead of these rags.
**Safiyyah**

*... and poverty is not evenly distributed across the UK.*

Children who grow up not just in poor families but in poor communities can face compounded disadvantage. Concentrations of poverty can affect expectations and opportunities, and the 'poverty of place' has played an important part in UK disadvantage[11].

Box 3 shows how child poverty is currently distributed across the UK. At country level, there are few differences: children in England, Scotland and Wales have similar chances of being poor. In Northern Ireland, which is not covered by the main data on poverty and

## Box 3: Child poverty in different parts of Britain

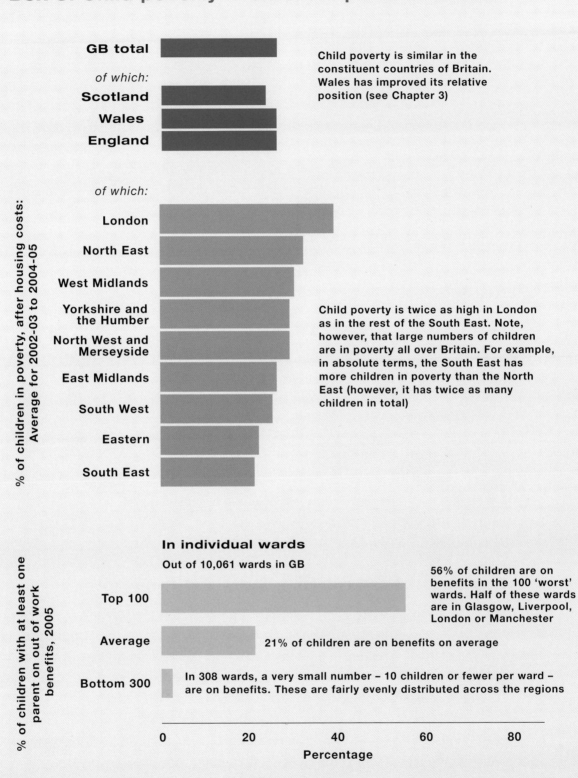

**% of children in poverty, after housing costs: Average for 2002-03 to 2004-05**

GB total

of which:

Scotland

Wales

England

Child poverty is similar in the constituent countries of Britain. Wales has improved its relative position (see Chapter 3)

of which:

London

North East

West Midlands

Yorkshire and the Humber

North West and Merseyside

East Midlands

South West

Eastern

South East

Child poverty is twice as high in London as in the rest of the South East. Note, however, that large numbers of children are in poverty all over Britain. For example, in absolute terms, the South East has more children in poverty than the North East (however, it has twice as many children in total)

**% of children with at least one parent on out of work benefits, 2005**

**In individual wards**

Out of 10,061 wards in GB

Top 100

56% of children are on benefits in the 100 'worst' wards. Half of these wards are in Glasgow, Liverpool, London or Manchester

Average

21% of children are on benefits on average

Bottom 300

In 308 wards, a very small number – 10 children or fewer per ward – are on benefits. These are fairly evenly distributed across the regions

0      20      40      60      80

Percentage

Source: Data on wards supplied to author by the DWP

cannot therefore be included in the modelling in Chapter 4, the problem may be worse[12]. Thirty-two per cent of children in Northern Ireland live in households whose only income comes from benefits, compared to 19 per cent in the rest of the UK. Combined with a high incidence of low pay, this makes the problem substantially harder to solve in this part of the UK, particularly through an over-emphasis on 'welfare to work' policies[13].

At regional level there are important differences, even away from the specific circumstances of London that makes it the hardest hit 'region'. Yet even though the average risk of poverty varies across regions, the 3.4 million children in poverty are not concentrated in any one part of the country, and many live in generally affluent regions. On the other hand, there is a stark contrast between specific neighbourhoods where the majority of children are poor and others where few or none live in poverty.

*"Poverty affects your lifestyle and makes you depressed. It is unhealthy for children to see their parents in that state. I went without antidepressants for a long time but am now on them. I always wanted to be able to cope, but it is difficult when your child starts demanding toys that cost £50. I want more for my son – I do not want to have to scrimp and scrape. School trips are also expensive – I had to pay £26 for one recently. I had to pay £18 for a sweatshirt with a logo on it for PE." (parent at Sheffield feedback event)*

*"Our school has got school uniform, but [our] council have slashed the school uniform grant. You cannot get a clothing grant anymore." (parent at London feedback event)*

*"The stigma your kids feel … you feel as if you're punishing the kids, but when you've £2 a day for food sometimes you just can't get it." (parent at Glasgow feedback event)*

## The social cost of child poverty, today and tomorrow

### *Child poverty harms society both psychologically and materially ...*
In addition to the suffering of individuals, child poverty brings widespread costs to our society. Some of these costs are immediate and direct, such as the resources devoted to helping families with housing difficulties, or to supporting children's needs through social services. Others are encountered over many years and even generations, as the damage done to children growing up in poverty has consequences that continue through their lives and potentially affect their own children's lives too. There also direct, tangible costs to society in terms of spending on problems associated with child poverty and revenue foregone from lost economic potential.

### *... due to its many knock-on effects ...*
It is not easy to measure the overall cost of not ending child poverty. The following figure categorises some of the short and long-term costs to individuals and to society, and suggests how they are related to each other.

**Figure 4** The cost of not ending child poverty
– a simplified map

| | 'INTERNAL COSTS'<br>Individual disadvantage<br>and hardship | 'EXTERNAL COSTS'<br>Consequences for society and for<br>social spending |
|---|---|---|
| **Impact of poverty in childhood** | • Child material and social hardship<br><br>• Knock-on effect on development during childhood | • Extra spending on child problems – eg behavioural, health, remedial education<br><br>• Implications of damage to families – extra services, knock on problems in schools, spending on protective care, antisocial behaviours |
| | **Outcomes**<br>e.g. educational, employment, psychological | |
| **Future consequences** | • Greater chance of material hardship in adulthood, linked to continuing economic disadvantage<br><br>• Knock-on effects on eg health, psychological well being, ability to achieve life goals<br><br>• Consequences for own children | • Extra spending on long-term consequences of child poverty eg poor health, higher crime<br><br>• Reduced economic capacity resulting from failure of individuals to reach potential<br><br>• Further spending on poverty caused by continuing cycle of disadvantage carried across generations |

Figure 4 illustrates how the immediate private suffering of a child living in a poor family has knock-on effects for individual outcomes later in childhood and in adulthood, and also how each of these outcomes can bring costs to society. This is because while growing up poor does not automatically make children into delinquents or prevent them from becoming useful and productive members of society, the experience of poverty increases the risk of encountering various difficulties in childhood and in later life. A key factor here is the influence of family environment on children's development. The Commission on Families and the Wellbeing of Children has concluded from the research evidence that "Poverty does matter, not so much because it directly causes children to have problems, but because it makes good family functioning more difficult to achieve."[14]

> "Childhood cannot be relived. Isolation, desperation and hurt are not just words for young people – they have a scarring impact. It is unforgivable that these years can be allowed to be stolen from young people through poverty." (small group session at Belfast feedback event)

*... and the financial cost, though hard to measure, is certainly large ...*

Some examples of tangible costs to society of problems to which child poverty makes a significant contribution are[15]:

- the £3 billion a year spent by local authority social services directed at children, of which more than £1 billion goes to residential provision;
- over £500 million a year spent directly on homeless families with children;
- an estimated £3.6 billion a year spent on children with special educational needs, some of which comprise social, emotional and behavioural difficulties;
- about £300 million a year spent on free school dinners;
- extra spending on primary health care for deprived children, potentially of the order of £500 million a year;
- knock-on costs in lost taxes from, and extra benefits for, adults with poor job prospects linked to educational failure in childhood. For example, the fiscal costs of labour market outcomes for those who are not in education, employment or training aged 16-18 are estimated at above £10 billion over the lifetime of a two-year cohort.

## Box 4: The reality of child poverty: (C) The cost to society

A report by the charity Barnado's[16] has looked at the stories of eight young people whose childhoods were wrecked by poverty. All had had chaotic lives blighted by the interaction of poverty with family difficulties. Keith had grown up with an alcoholic father, Louise felt unwanted and worthless and Maria's family faced homelessness and destitution after its application for asylum was refused. For none of these young people was poverty alone the root cause of their difficulties, but for all, it exacerbated their problems. The report argued that early intervention could have prevented their lives from entering a downward spiral, which had led for example to truancy, crime and drug abuse. In fact, the failure to intervene early had eventually led to tens of thousands of pounds being spent on each them – and hundreds of thousands in the case of those going into local authority care.

*... while the intergenerational effects seem to be growing.*

The last of the above costs is an example of how poor children who fail to reach their potential in childhood can have sustained poor outcomes in adulthood. Recent research shows that the experience of growing up poor has an influence on the chance of being poor as an adult independently of other features of family background – with the effect continuing beyond young adulthood and into middle age[17]. Most worryingly, this effect appears to have strengthened for cohorts who were poor as teenagers in the 1980s compared to teenagers in the 1970s. Specifically, the extent to which teenage poverty can predict poverty in one's early thirties has doubled between these two cohorts. For the later group, adult experiences such as lone parenthood, unemployment and economic inactivity have become more common, and these factors are closely associated with the extra risk of poverty felt by those who grew up poor. In other words, in a changing world, adults who were poor as children are being exposed to new risks. As those who end up poor have children of their own, the cycle continues. Unless this cycle is broken, the result is likely to be a worsening from one generation to the next both in the overall scale and in the concentration of poverty and associated difficulties: a dynamic of social polarisation that becomes increasingly hard to break.

## International comparisons

*Most other countries have fewer poor children than the UK ...*

Child poverty in the UK is at far higher levels than in most comparable countries. In the 25 countries of the EU, only Italy, Portugal and the Slovak Republic have higher percentages of children living on incomes below 60 per cent of the median. Even though in some poorer EU countries this threshold implies lower absolute living standards than in the UK, this demonstrates that the UK has an income distribution that is skewed against the poorest to an atypical degree. Moreover, UK child poverty is higher than in European countries with similar levels of affluence: in 2003, about 50 per cent higher than in France, and more than twice as high as in the Scandinavian countries[18]. While these disparities are today smaller than in the mid-1990s, because the recent fall in child poverty in the UK has not generally been matched elsewhere, child poverty here remains a long way above the norm.

*... and child poverty has not grown and surpassed adult rates everywhere ...*

The UK's experience of a large rise in child poverty since 1980, to well above the adult rate, is not a universal pattern. Some countries like the Netherlands have seen rapid rises in youth poverty, and some like Canada and the United States have substantially higher youth rates than adult rates. On the other hand, countries like Norway, Sweden and Ireland saw a fall, rather than a rise, in child poverty in the last two decades of the 20th century, and in these countries children are not more likely to be poor than adults[19].

*... because more children elsewhere have a parent who works, typically in a less unequal labour market than the UK's, and redistribution in the UK is weaker.*

Three aspects of UK experience appear to explain much of the difference with other countries:

> **The large proportion of children living in households without work.** This has fallen from one in five to one in six children, but remains higher in the UK than in any other EU country. In France and Germany, whose unemployment rates are double the UK's, only about one child in six lives in a workless household[20]. Two thirds of the UK's children in workless households have lone parents. Lone parenthood is more common in the UK than in other European countries, and lone parents are less likely to be in work[21].

- **Pay inequality affecting those whose parents do work.** Wage and earnings inequalities widened rapidly in the UK from 1975 to 2000, with, for example, the ratio of the top to the bottom decile of male wages rising from 2.8 to 4.2[22]. On the other hand, earnings inequalities were stable during the 1980s and 1990s in countries like Finland and Germany, where they had already been lower than in the UK. They were also stable in France, where earnings were slightly less equal than in the UK in the early 1980s but were much more equal by the mid-1990s (OECD *Employment Outlook*, 2004, p. 141).

- **A less redistributive tax and benefits system than in many countries.** Figure 5 shows that while the effect of employment and earnings patterns creates relatively high child poverty in the UK before the state intervenes, in these terms it is not exceptional, with seven other EU countries having higher rates. However, the UK does less than most other countries to redistribute income

**Figure 5** Child poverty rate before and after cash benefits

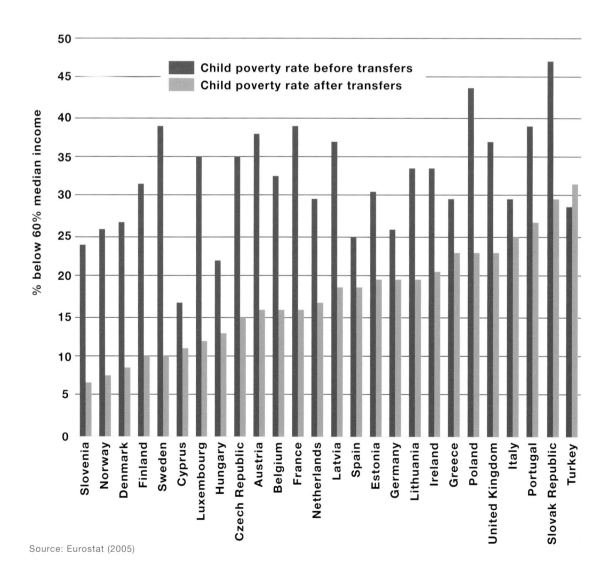

Source: Eurostat (2005)

through cash benefits. A particularly striking contrast is with Sweden, the only country with more children in lone-parent families than the UK. Sweden has a slightly higher child poverty rate before redistribution, but less than half the rate after redistribution. In recent years the UK has increased the generosity of payments for poor children more than most other countries, but with a starting point of lower levels of out-of-work benefits and lower universal payments for children, it has a long way to go to catch up.

Thus, international experience shows that the high levels of child poverty in the UK are not inevitable, but have deep-rooted causes, so that bringing our levels down to international benchmarks will be far from easy.

# 2 The challenge of finding a comprehensive solution

*Tackling poverty involves not just direct transfers of income, but also improving opportunities and environments for low income families.*

A straightforward way of abolishing child poverty would be to set tax credits and benefits at levels that mean that no child needs to live in a household with below 60 per cent median income. This would address the immediate problem of improving the material circumstances of deprived children. However, it would have a high public cost (see Chapter 4), and would not tackle the underlying causes of poverty or of the problems that surround it. A more comprehensive solution needs to address a range of factors that may affect children's wellbeing and development. These include parents' employment patterns, the quality of childcare, the availability of suitable housing, educational opportunities and the characteristics of local communities.

An improvement of family opportunities needs to be at the heart of any solution – opening up new possibilities for both parents and children. These can influence both the immediate material wellbeing of the family and the longer-term development of the child. This chapter considers three central influences on adult and child opportunity: employment, education and childcare; and also the role of direct support for family incomes. The following chapter goes on to identify the contribution made by some of these factors in reducing child poverty over the past few years.

The following analysis does not cover wider influences on children's development, including features of their environment such as housing and communities. These have important but hard to measure influences on child poverty. The analysis of such influences is beyond the scope of this report.

## Work chances, work patterns and child poverty

*Work is the most reliable single route out of poverty ...*

A child living in a household where nobody works has a three in four chance of being in poverty. For those in a household with a mixture of working and non-working adults, the probability reduces to one in three, and where all adults are working, to one in eight. No other factor is such a strong predictor of whether a child is poor. It is therefore unsurprising that 'work is the best route out of poverty' has been a central tenet of anti-poverty strategies. This does not, however, imply that the solution to child poverty is for every parent to work (see Box 5).

**Box 5: Limits to a work-based solution**

This chapter inevitably has a lot to say about the role of work opportunities in helping to reduce child poverty. Improving the chance of parents to earn money is at the heart of an 'active' solution to low family income, alongside the 'passive' remedy of giving poor families more money in benefits and tax credits.

Yet this does not mean that the only way to help children is for all their parents to go out to work. In feedback events held with families living on low incomes and local service providers as part of this project, there was broad consensus about the importance of parents being able to make choices about the balance between working to support their children and staying at home to look after them. Supporting this choice relies first and foremost on providing adequate out-of-work incomes that does not mean that work is the only alternative to poverty (see the last section in this chapter). But choice is also a matter of the kinds of work opportunities that are available. The chance to work appropriate hours, to obtain good childcare arrangements and to have flexibility around the needs of raising a family can be at least as important as the opportunity to get some kind of job. Governments cannot control these conditions, but can work hard to promote them.

*"We discussed the fact that it should be important for parents to retain choice. It should not simply be that work is the only route out of poverty. Parents should have a choice about when they feel work is the right step for them to take. We were concerned about the pressure that is being put on parents, particularly lone parents, to move back into employment very early. Maybe they feel they are not ready to take the step and that their children's needs at that point might not be best met by returning to employment." (small group session at London feedback event)*

*"All my tax credits and most of my wages go to keeping my four kids; they're in three different kinds of childcare and I've been working for six years and I'm not any better off for working. I'm playing at being an employee and playing at being a mum – can't do either fully." (parent at Glasgow feedback event)*

*... but the nature and rhythm of work opportunities matter greatly.*

On the other hand, it is not the case that when a parent gets a job, his or her family's poverty permanently disappears. Today, even with a generous regime of in-work tax credits for families with children, half of all children in poverty have at least one parent in work. Low pay is one contributing factor: while only one in 20 employees overall are in poor households, for employees with low hourly pay, the risk is one in seven[23]. Another important influence is the amount of work within the family. Of 1.9 million children who are in poverty despite having at least one working parent, only 100,000 are in families where all adults are in full-time work[24].

Thus, while it matters greatly to children's experience of poverty whether any of their parents are working, the characteristics of parents' experiences in the labour market also matter: whether they get better-paying jobs, their hours of work and whether their work is stable or erratic. A recent study for Save the Children on factors affecting severe and persistent poverty concluded that while long periods of worklessness are associated with persistent poverty, the most severe poverty is particularly associated with instability in employment status[25]. Where members of a household make transitions in and out of work, there is a strong risk of a period with low or no income. Part of the solution to this problem lies in a smoother tax and benefits system, but improvements in job retention would also help families greatly.

> *"You go back to work and the first thing they do is take your benefit away ... your back to work adviser didn't calculate that in!" (small group session at Glasgow feedback event)*

### One factor is low work rates for lone parents ...

An important factor underlying the relatively high incidence of child poverty in the UK is the situation of their parents, a high proportion of whom face barriers to employment. In particular, over four in ten children living in poverty have lone parents, and of these, nearly 80 per cent are not working. Some lone parents give priority to staying at home to look after their children, and in this sense it is the UK's high rate of lone parenthood that produces non-working families. But lone parents' low employment rate, by international standards, can also be attributed to barriers to employment. Part of this is due to this group's relatively high likelihood of having characteristics associated with a lower chance of working: they are more likely to have low qualifications, to be claiming sickness and disability benefits and to live in social housing than other adults of their age[26]. Part is due to practical barriers such as a lack of acceptable childcare options.

The overall result is that a child with a lone parent is over five times as likely to have no earnings coming into his or her family than a child with two parents, and has only a 20 per cent chance of having a parent with full-time earnings. Moreover, while lone parents' entry rate into employment is now as high as for other people not working, their exit rate remains twice the average. Thus, lone parents more than other groups are finding it hard to access stable jobs, and/or are finding it hard to hold down a job given other pressures in their lives and the practicalities of childcare.

### ... but a neglected factor has been high poverty rates among single-earner couples ...

Even though the vast majority of couples with children are now in work, this does not mean that they have escaped poverty. One and a quarter million children living with couples in work are still poor, about twice as many as in non-working couples and a similar number as in non-working lone-parent families. Thus, there is as much potential to reduce poverty by improving the incomes of working couples as by moving lone parents into work. Yet there has been much less focus on this task. As argued elsewhere in this report, there is an argument for improving the relative value of in-work tax credits for this group. But there is also a need to do more to help improve working opportunities for second earners. Most poor working couples with children either have only one earner or are self-employed.

*... while disability and mental illness play important roles ...*

A less well-recognised factor affecting parental employment chances is the fact that many parents have mental and physical disabilities and illnesses that affect their ability to work. The Department for Work and Pensions' analysis of its clients shows that over 900,000 children are in families where at least one parent claims a benefit due to a disability. A wide range of conditions, ranging from severe physical impairments to stress-related illnesses, have impacts on parental work prospects and hence on child poverty.

One particular issue of concern is mental illness. There is a lack of hard data, but it is likely that approximately 1.25 million children in England and Wales live with parents or carers who have a mental health problem, while only one in four people with mental health problems are in employment. The evidence shows that poverty and mental health difficulties interact, with the stresses caused by poverty contributing to the onset of conditions such as depression, while the employment impacts of mental illness can in turn accentuate poverty. This interaction seems to affect lone parents in particular, who face a greater challenge in bringing up children in difficult circumstances. Lone parents are two to three times as likely to experience the most common mental disorders than parents in couples with children[27]. Another important feature of mental illness is its unpredictability, which contributes to the unstable work patterns that can contribute to severe child poverty, as described above.

*... and government now has a range of tools to help improve parental employment rates.*

The government has put considerable stress on a range of policies to improve employment outcomes for parents. These include:

- measures to help people into jobs, such as the New Deal for Lone Parents;
- measures to encourage people actively to consider work, notably the development of work-focused interviews and of personal advisers;
- measures to make work pay, notably the development of in-work tax credits, especially for families with children, and the introduction and raising of the National Minimum Wage;
- improvements in the supply of childcare as well as help in financing it through the tax credit system; and
- piloted measures to give more intensive support to people, before or after entering jobs, to help progress into and within the labour market. The Pathways to Work pilots give intensive help to disabled people. The Employee Retention and Advancement demonstration project is exploring more generally how employment services can help people towards sustainable employment.

Chapter 3 considers the impact that some of these measures have had so far on child poverty. One notable feature of the policy strategy is that it has so far been better designed to move individuals into work than to transform the labour market. Providing job search help and 'making work pay' through tax credits can help greatly in the short term to move people into jobs, but do not in themselves ensure that jobs are worthwhile, well-paid or sustainable. Measures to help individuals to do better in the labour market remain at an underdeveloped, experimental stage. Thus, while the present policy armoury does contain a wide range of tools, it does not yet provide a comprehensive, long-term solution to improve the position of parents in the labour market and thus permanently reduce child poverty.

*"Not enough is done to recognise what it means to move from benefits into a job and the barrier they face – ie fear of taking a job and it not working out. A flexible benefits system would help so that if a person is unable to do a job (for example if they have a disability) they can move back to benefits without having to wait weeks for claims to be processed.... People need the opportunity to 'test jobs'. Fear is still a barrier to returning to or taking work." (small group session at Liverpool feedback event)*

*"If parents are working very hard in a job, what is the point if there are no cheap or good-quality youth clubs or childcare centres? These keep their children off the streets and away from the effects of poverty, such as crime, drugs and bullying. We must address these issues together and understand their roots in poverty if we want to end child poverty." (parent at London feedback event)*

## Education at the heart of a long-term solution

*Overall, improved education is essential to the longer-term fight against poverty and disadvantage.*

One feature of a long-term solution is to ensure that parents today and in the future have the skills needed to access good quality jobs. This can be achieved through improvements in education and training both for adults and for children. In particular, a more inclusive education system could help reduce the persistence of poverty across generations, as disadvantaged children fail to access the educational opportunities that could help them avoid poverty when they are themselves parents.

*Spending extra years at school clearly improves wage and employment prospects ...*

Overall, there is powerful evidence that education in childhood and youth improves one's chances in adulthood. This applies both to employment effects – how much time one spends working rather than not working, and to wage effects – average pay when in work. Moreover, research[28] indicates that this return is likely to be high at the margin for vulnerable groups likely to leave education early:

- for people leaving school around the minimum age, each extra year of schooling appears to boost earnings in mid-life by about 15 per cent;
- extra educational qualifications boost expected earnings for people from disadvantaged backgrounds at least as much as for those from better-off backgrounds (the premium for women is similar regardless of background; for men it is higher for the disadvantaged);
- while lower-level vocational qualifications have no discernible impact on wages, they have a dramatic impact on job prospects: male employment rates aged 23-25 rise from 68 per cent for the unqualified to 75 per cent for those with Level 1 and 89 per cent with Level 2 qualifications;
- acquiring basic literacy and numeracy skills also boosts the probability of employment. For example, people with Level 1 numeracy are about five percentage points more likely to be employed than those without, and 2-3 percentage points more likely after correcting for associated factors[29];
- evidence on the impact of learning in adulthood is less definitive. It appears to show that for unqualified adults, some forms of learning in mid-life can be highly beneficial to income, but the evidence does not allow a generalised gain to be measured.

### ... and both education and the income that it brings feed into better outcomes for the next generation ...

In families where parents have good jobs and strong educational backgrounds, children tend to do better at school. It is hard to distinguish educational and income effects, but the evidence shows that each has some independent influence. For example[30]:

- An increase in income of one third of the mean (that is, an increase of about £140 per week) increases the probability of achieving five or more GCSEs at A*-C by an estimated 3 to 4 percentage points and increases the probability of achieving a degree by a similar magnitude.
- One extra year of a mother's education increases her child's probability of staying on in school beyond minimum school leaving by 8 to 10 percentage points.

These substantial effects illustrate how breaking a cycle of poverty and low educational attainment can help reduce family poverty from one generation to the next.

### ... but targeted policy measures remain under-developed.

In light of the above evidence, it is clear that a long-term assault on child poverty needs to involve measures to improve educational opportunities for disadvantaged children. Governments put a high priority on raising educational performance generally, and have also developed certain measures to give extra help to certain groups or communities. These include area initiatives such as Education Action Zones and measures to help people on low incomes such as financial support for those continuing in further or higher education. Other initiatives have targeted adults with low skills for extra help.

However, such programmes are often on the margins of policies to improve educational outcomes – for example, the amount devoted to Education Action Zones represents only a minute fraction of all spending on education. Most money for schools is directly proportional to the number of students, regardless of their backgrounds. There is some evidence that programmes giving financial support to 16-year-olds to stay at school or to lower-income groups to participate in higher education can yield positive outcomes. In particular, evaluation of Educational Maintenance Allowances shows that they have succeeded in improving staying-on rates. What is less evident, however, is that effective ways have been found to help children growing up in poverty to thrive during the compulsory school years. Even the limited experiment of Education Action Zones has not had clear-cut positive impacts. We thus lack a good understanding of what works in targeted interventions to help economically disadvantaged children in primary and secondary education.

## Childcare and opportunities for parents and children

*Families can benefit from better quality, more accessible and more plentiful childcare ...*

Improvements in childcare can have a dual impact on child poverty. In the short term, they can help enable parents to work; in the much longer term, good quality early childhood experiences can contribute to child development and hence improve children's lifetime prospects.

Strategies to improve childcare opportunities have had a number of dimensions, including:

- improvement of provision, through measures to increase supply, using a mixture of providers;
- improvement of access, particularly through tax credits that subsidise most of the cost for low-income families in work;
- the establishment of multipurpose children's services focused on deprived communities, particularly Children's Centres and other Sure Start services.

*"Free or subsidised quality childcare should be available and open to all children including children with a disability." (small group session at Belfast feedback event)*

*... but despite progress, shortfalls in provision still contribute to child poverty.*

These measures undoubtedly help improve opportunities for many families. Yet an assessment of their contribution to overcoming child poverty[31] concludes that there remain serious shortfalls, and raises doubts over what the promise of moving towards 'universal' provision will mean in practice, given that Children's Centres will be sited in every 'community' but carry no guarantee of offering options to each individual.

Many parents still do not feel that they have a good quality childcare option that they are happy with. In its public consultations in the course of this project, the Joseph Rowntree Foundation noted a widespread view that improvements in childcare, although welcome, were not enough to meet the requirements of parents who would like to work. A host of difficulties are still encountered in different combinations by many parents, including: lack of available childcare with which parents feel comfortable, the continued high cost of provision even after the subsidy, inflexibility of arrangements to pay the supporting tax credit, the lack of resources to compensate friends and relatives who might care for children and difficulties around the hours and working arrangements offered by employers. Above all, parents want choice over their work and childcare package. This will not automatically be provided by a network of centres offering 'wrap-around' institutional childcare, since many parents prioritise seeing their children after school rather than picking them up in the evening.

## The structure of income transfers and the structure of poverty

*A key factor will be the level of benefits and tax credits, for different family types.*

The above discussion illustrates how a strategy to eliminate child poverty can include measures to improve family opportunities. But however much these improve, not all families will be able to escape poverty without financial help from the state. Some will remain outside work, and others have earnings that do not meet their needs. Therefore, the structure of support, both inside and outside employment, will continue to have a crucial effect on child poverty rates.

Much will depend on the generosity of the system: on what can be afforded overall, in terms of the level of the main benefits and tax credits going to poor families. But the *structure* of entitlements is also crucial. How much are different kinds of family entitled to? Future benefit and tax credit rates are based partly on the current structure as it is carried forward, but also to a great extent on the way in which different entitlements are uprated. At present, this varies greatly for different components of family income. For example, the child element of the Child Tax Credit is rising at least in line with average earnings, Child Benefit is rising in line with prices and the family element of the Child Tax Credit is not rising at all.

In the years ahead, the structure of income transfers will affect the structure of poverty and the rate of its reduction in a number of ways, notably the following:

*The balance between in- and out-of-work support: to eradicate child poverty, non-working incomes in particular need to rise.*

Minimum incomes are bound to be lower for non-working households than for those with jobs: the government is careful to ensure that there remains a financial incentive to work. At present, the consequence is that nearly three in four children in families not in work are in poverty, whereas the chances are much lower for families in work, even those where all workers are low paid. For example, a lone parent with a low-paid job has a one in five chance of being below 60 per cent median income, even though their pay alone almost never (in only 4 per cent of cases) brings them above this level. The addition of tax credits and benefits is enough to bring about half of these low-paid lone parents out of poverty, and a further one in four escape poverty when other sources of income are added in[32]. The role of tax credits has become ever more important in this equation, and low-paid lone parents working more than the 16 hours required to qualify for the Working Tax Credit have only an 8 per cent chance of being poor.

It could thus be argued that in future, raising out-of-work benefits, relative to average incomes, will be the crucial long-term change if child poverty is eventually to be eliminated. However, to preserve work incentives, it may be necessary to raise in-work support as well. Moreover, since 2003 the fortunes of children in families in and out of work have to some extent been locked together through the Child Tax Credit, a key component in the income of both groups. Nevertheless, the other components should not be neglected. In particular, Income Support, the benefit providing for the basic needs of most out-of-work parents, is only being uprated with prices. This means that the total income of many non-working families may, under present policies, not even keep pace with average incomes, let alone improve relative to the median.

Lone parents compared to couples: many working couples need a lot of extra help to escape poverty.

A further crucial dimension is family type. Although children with lone parents are more likely to be poor because their parents are less likely to work, a child in a workless household has the same chance (72 per cent) of being poor with two parents as with one. Moreover, where parents are working but in part-time or low-paid jobs, the tax credit system is arguably more favourable to lone parents than to couples. It is much more likely to take a lone parent who works full time out of poverty than a couple where one person works full time, and the same is true when comparing a single part-time worker in these two family types. This may be seen as fair, since a couple has more scope to add a second income, and a lone parent may find it harder to work full time. Nevertheless, it is notable that over 80 per cent of poor children with working parents live in couple families, and that a couple with children where a man is low paid is nearly twice as likely to be poor than a family with a lone mother[33]. Thus, future reductions in in-work child poverty could depend to a considerable degree on the generosity of the tax credit system to couples. (See, however, Box 6.)

## Box 6: Equivalence scales, poverty and the tax/benefits system

The calculations about poverty reduction made in the present report use the standard definitions of income poverty (see Box 1 above), with adjustments for family need based on the official 'equivalence scales'. These start with a couple as a standard unit, and make adjustments for family composition to calculate the poverty line for each family. For example, when calculating poverty after housing costs, the scales subtract 45 per cent for a household with a single adult and add between 18 per cent and 28 per cent, rising with age, for each child between ages 2 and 16. However, benefits and tax credits do not systematically assume that needs vary according to these scales. For example:

- Per-child benefits and credits are not weighted according to age. But the poverty measure assumes that older children need more. So a family on benefits is more likely to be judged poor the older its children.
- The arrival of the first child raises benefit entitlements much more than that of subsequent children. But the poverty measure assumes that each child needs the same. So a family living on benefits is more likely to be considered poor if it has, say, four children than if it has only one. In particular, having one extra older child brings in less extra benefit income than the presumed needs of that child[34].
- Working families get a tax credit to help with adult needs that is the same for a couple or a lone parent, even though the poverty measure assumes that a couple needs substantially more. This partially explains the higher poverty risks of working couples.

In presenting below the measures needed to reduce poverty using current equivalence scales, this report is not seeking to make judgements about the actual relative needs of different families. If these were to be deemed different from the arbitrary weightings used in the scales, the design of solutions would be somewhat different.

Large families: families with more children are at greater risk.

The risk of a child living in poverty rises substantially if he or she has more than one sibling. The poverty rate rises to 50 per cent for those living in the largest families, with four or more children, compared to 23 per cent for those in one- or two-child families. In couples, the number of children is particularly significant, with only about one in seven children being poor in one- or two-child families, but nearly a third of children in larger ones[35].

There may be a number of causes of these differences, not all related to differences in the tax credit and benefit system. For example, it may be harder for both people in a couple to work where there are more children, with the cost of childcare a major factor, and families where only one person in a couple works have a high poverty risk. It is also possible that people with some characteristics associated with a higher risk of poverty, such as socioeconomic background, are also more likely on average to have larger families. However, a significant factor is that tax credits and benefits are more likely to compensate fully for the assumed extra cost of a first child than of subsequent children (see Box 6 above). A restructuring of these entitlements could help to bring poverty numbers down.

Universal and targeted benefits: not all payments to help end child poverty will necessarily be narrowly targeted.

A final important feature of the tax and benefit system in addressing child poverty is the degree to which it gives entitlements to all families or only those with low incomes. Child Benefit and the family element of Child Tax Credit go to most families. They remain significant in boosting family incomes, but are presently declining relative to average income. An extra pound of public spending will go further towards reducing poverty if it is paid in income-tested benefits. However, insofar as 'progressive universalism' (something for every family but more for the least well off) helps maintain widespread public support for public transfers to families, maintaining universal benefits helps in the long term to prevent poverty. Moreover, universal payments have better take-up and are easier to claim, which also adds to their effectiveness. As shown in Chapter 4, there can be a role for these payments in an anti-poverty strategy that is nevertheless cost-effective.

# 3 Progress so far, and what remains undone

## Child poverty trends, 1999-2005

*A steady fall in child poverty has benefited some groups more than others.*
Child poverty has fallen or remained steady in each year since 1998/99. Although by 2004/05 it had dropped by less than the target of a quarter, the fall was nearly one fifth on the after housing cost measure (see Figure 6) and close to the target of one quarter before housing costs. This fall represents a historic reversal of a trend in the other direction over the previous 20 years. It is particularly significant that relative poverty fell at a time when average incomes, and hence the threshold at which poverty is defined, were rising rapidly. The poverty line in 2004/05 was 21 per cent higher in real terms than in 1998/99, equivalent to £47 a week more after housing costs for a couple with two children.

This progress has been made partly by increasing the number of families with work, and partly by reducing the chances that various types of family, defined by their demographic characteristics and whether they are working or not, will find themselves poor. In particular,

**Figure 6** Percentage of children below 60% median income after housing costs

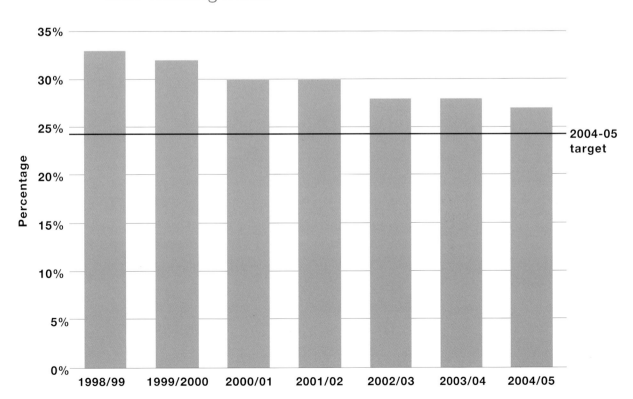

compared to the late 1990s, children with the following characteristics were significantly less likely to be poor[36]:

- **Children with lone parents,** whose risk of poverty has fallen from 61 per cent to 48 per cent, partly because their parents are more likely to be working, and partly because, working or not, they get more from the state. (For children living with couples, the chance of being poor has changed by less, but since there are more children in this situation, the effect has been substantial: see below.)
- **Children in families with under-5s,** whose risk of poverty has fallen faster than for older families: from 35 per cent to 29 per cent.
- **Children in families with disabled people**, whether disabled children or adults. In particular where a child is disabled the risk of having a low income is now 30 per cent rather than 40 per cent.
- **Children in Wales, and in some English regions**. A decade ago, child poverty was markedly higher in Wales than in England: 34 per cent rather than 31 per cent in 1994/95. Now the rate is the same in the two countries. From 1998/99 to 2004-05, when the child poverty rate fell by five percentage points across Britain, it fell by 11 percentage points in the North West, 11 in the North East and seven points in Scotland and in Wales. The target of a one quarter reduction was fulfilled in three English regions: the North East, the North West and the South West. In stark contrast, child poverty in London actually rose slightly during this period.

*"I am a lone parent, with a disabled child, on £190 a week, but I am still struggling. I cannot afford the things that my children want. I am desperate to work, but because of hospital appointments, jobs are not available. The hospital provides no childcare for my nine-year-old son. What will help me get out of this?... I can afford to travel to hospital, since my expenses are reimbursed, but while I am at the hospital, my children need feeding." (parent at Sheffield feedback event)*

## The relative importance of work, pay and redistribution

Three ways that a family might move out of poverty are by moving into work, by increasing their earnings or by receiving more in benefits or tax credits from the state.

*More children are living in families with work, and this has helped cut poverty...*

In recent years, the movement of parents into work has played an important part in the decline in child poverty. Since 1994, the number of children living in workless households has fallen by a quarter – around 600,000 children. Much emphasis has been put on the rapid rise in the lone-parent employment rate, from 45 per cent to 56 per cent so far under the present government. Another trend that has been just as important in terms of reducing the number of workless households is the declining number of couples without work. The proportion of children living with couples who had nobody working in their household almost halved from 1994 to 2005, from 11 per cent to 6 per cent.

At the same time, the chance of being poor can change for a child in a particular type of family, in terms of whether it contains a lone parent or a couple, and how many of its members work full or part time. For example, if lone parents in part-time work improve their pay, increase their working hours or receive more generous tax credits, poverty among this group may fall. Similarly, rises in out-of-work benefits may reduce the risk of poverty for workless families.

*... but whereas early signs were that rising employment was the most important factor ...*

How important in practice have these different factors been? An early analysis of reductions in child poverty under Labour, carried out by David Piachaud and Holly Sutherland in 2003, found that, between 1997 and 2001, rises in employment accounted for a fall of about 2 percentage points in child poverty, around half the actual observed reduction. Changes in earnings appeared to have had little influence, and this research suggested that tax and benefit increases had accounted for much of the remaining reduction. In other words, in the early years of the Labour government, movements back into work seemed to be at least as important as the growing generosity of tax credits and other tax and benefit measures, as a driver of child poverty reductions.

*... recently it appears that other factors such as tax credits have had a more direct impact ...*

The Institute for Fiscal Studies[37] (IFS) has recently calculated a breakdown of the drivers behind a more recent fall in child poverty – from 1998/99 to 2004/05. This looks at the relative influence of how many children are in different types of family and the risk of poverty in each family type – although it does not distinguish the extent to which this risk is affected by earnings levels and the amount transferred to and from the family in taxes and benefits. The most important influences identified by the IFS are shown in Figure 7 overleaf.

These breakdowns suggest that, for this later period, the biggest effects were not associated with movement into work but with the reduced risk of poverty within family types defined by their composition and work status. Only 120,000 of the 700,000 fall in child poverty in this period can be attributed directly to falls in worklessness. The new tax credit regime has brought substantial increases in out-of-work incomes for families with children, and although they are still far more likely than not to be in poverty, reductions in their poverty risk have caused nearly 200,000 fewer children to be below the poverty line.

But it is among certain in-work family types that the falling risk has been greatest. In 1998, the child of a lone parent was still almost as likely as not to be in poverty if the parent had a part-time job, but now the chance of escaping poverty through part-time work is almost three to one. The poverty risk for a child with one parent working and the other

**Figure 7** Six main changes that helped reduce child poverty by 700,000 from 1998/99 to 2004/05

| Change | | Consequence for child poverty |
|---|---|---|
| • The number of children with workless lone parents fell from 14% to 13% of all children | ➡ | – 60,000 |
| • The number of all children in workless couple families fell from 7% to 6% of all children | ➡ | – 63,000 |
| • The chance of being poor with a non-working lone parent fell from 79% to 72% | ➡ | – 107,000 |
| • The chance of being poor in a workless couple fell from 82% to 72% | ➡ | – 88,000 |
| • The chance of being poor with a lone parent working part time fell from 45% to 27% | ➡ | – 132,000 |
| • The chance of being poor in a couple with one full-time worker and the other not working fell from 28% to 21% | ➡ | – 154,000 |

not has fallen by less in percentage terms, but the larger number of such children means that the effect on the number in poverty is even greater. Between them the reduction in poverty risk in these two types of working family accounts for 40 per cent of the total reduction in child poverty. While this may potentially have been influenced by earnings, there is so far no evidence to show that this is the case[38]. On the other hand, the growing generosity of in-work tax credits was predicted by models to raise many working families with children across the poverty line. Indeed, the extent to which this has occurred is lower than forecast, and due to difficulties with the accuracy of surveys, these results must be seen as approximate[39].

*... and with worklessness now falling less quickly, movement into work can only be part of the picture ...*

Thus, while the early signs under the Labour government seemed to show that rising employment was the biggest factor behind falls in child poverty, more recently it appears that jobs played a smaller role, and rises in tax credits a relatively large one. The decline in worklessness has slowed: according to the Labour Force Survey, the number of children in non-working families fell by 300,000 from Spring 1997 to Spring 2001, but only by 100,000 in the following four-year period, to Spring 2005. Rising employment rates for lone parents have not slowed, but the sharp fall in worklessness among couples with children during the 1990s appears to have halted[40]. Moreover, the reduction in the *percentage* of lone parents not working has been partly offset by an increase in the *number* of children in lone-parent families, by about 150,000 between 1998/99 and 2004/05, to rise above 3 million for the first time. The increased likelihood that children would have a lone parent, with a higher risk of poverty, added about 50,000 to the number in poverty[41].

What is the scope for further falls in worklessness, and how much might this contribute to the reduction in poverty? Figures 8a and 8b overleaf indicate that in the past decade children in workless families have increasingly been concentrated in lone-parent families, and that most of those living with couples now have at least one disabled parent. Thus, the main scope for further reductions in worklessness is likely to come from increases in lone parents' employment, but here too there are limits. Four in ten children of lone parents are either under 5 or have a parent claiming disability benefits. Many others have young siblings; half of all lone parents on Income Support have at least one child under 5 and 80 per cent at least one child under 11[42].

This does not mean that getting families back into work should stop being a central part of the fight to end child poverty. Even if moves into work can only play a partial role in this process, for many families this will be a crucial step in a longer-term trajectory that at best will improve their incomes and living standards. Moreover, for each person who moves into work, there is (in most cases) a substantial gain for the public purse that can potentially be reinvested in cutting poverty in other ways, such as raising benefits.

However, such efforts should acknowledge that welfare to work will in future require considerable personal support, to people who are likely to have a combination of disadvantages in entering the labour market. Many of those consulted by the Joseph Rowntree Foundation in this project emphasised that getting into sustainable employment can be a long drawn-out process requiring a lot of advice, support and preparation. This will require a huge investment in advisers and other personnel.

*"The Pathways to Work approach piloted in some areas of the country has been very successful; we have no evidence it is going wrong and we very much endorse the strategy. However, if they are to be rolled out across the country they must be properly resourced, which does not sit well with heavy job cuts at DWP. If initiatives like Pathways to Work are to be implemented, they must use properly trained advisers whose workload is realistic." (advice worker at London feedback event)*

Moreover, the numbers show that even if 'work is the best route out of poverty', reducing worklessness can only be part of the story of achieving aggregate reductions in the child poverty rate. To put these numbers in perspective, the number of children in workless

**43**

**Figure 8a** The number of children in workless households has fallen by a quarter in one decade. Most such children now have lone parents

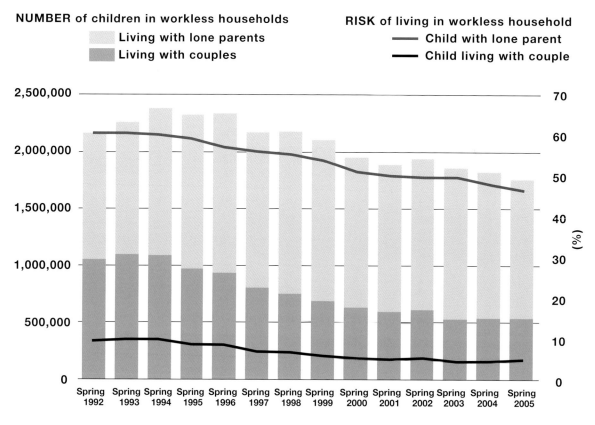

NUMBER of children in workless households
  Living with lone parents
  Living with couples

RISK of living in workless household
  —— Child with lone parent
  —— Child living with couple

- The chance of a child of a lone parent being in a workless household has fallen from 62% to 48%. For couples it has fallen from 11% to 6%.

- Seven in ten children in workless families now have lone parents, compared to only half in the early 1990s.

families fell by about 75,000 a year from 1997 to 2001 and by 25,000 from 2001 to 2005, but child poverty must fall by an average of about 200,000 a year to keep on track to meet government targets.

*... so levels of earnings, tax credits and benefits have become crucial.*
Thus, ongoing reductions in child poverty depend not just on how many children have parents in work, but also on the chance of children in workless families being poor and the chance of children in working families being poor. With about half of poor children currently having parents in work, these are of equal importance. Specifically, the following factors influence poverty risk:

  ■ Whether benefit and tax credit levels give those without earnings sufficient income to rise above the poverty line. Although as noted above the risk of child poverty without work in the family has fallen, benefits still fall well short of providing 60 per cent median income for most children. Many who do escape poverty without work in the family are likely to have other adults in the household who are earning.

## Figure 8b Half of children in workless families either have a disabled parent or are under 5 and have a lone parent

**Children in families receiving key out-of-work benefits (2005)**

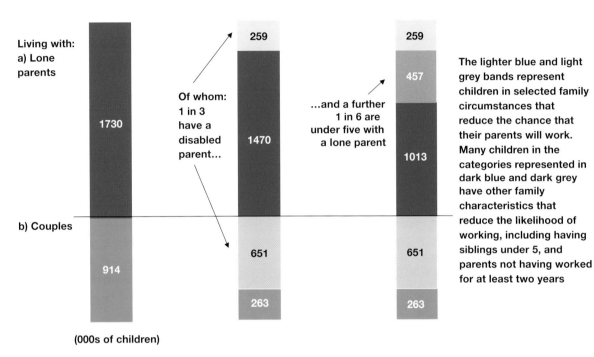

(000s of children)

Source: DWP client group analysis

- Whether tax credits are enough to raise incomes of people in work above the poverty line. The sharp hikes in tax credits in recent years, and especially in 2003, appear to have contributed to substantial reductions in poverty risk for some groups, especially for lone parents working part time.

- The number of hours worked in a working family. Despite in-work tax credits, children with parents who work part time, and those living with couples of whom only one is working, have much higher poverty risks than others in working families. In-work child poverty remains high partly because many parents returning to work have moved into jobs with short hours and low pay. One neglected route out of poverty is for the non-working partner of a working parent to get a part-time job: this reduces the poverty risk from one in five to one in 16.

- Pay rates among parents near the bottom of the labour market. In couples in particular, people with low pay have a high chance of remaining in poverty[43]. Improvements in the pay of low-paid parents would both raise some people above the poverty line and reduce the tax credit bill, releasing public resources that could be used in other ways to tackle child poverty.

## Public policy levers: what remains undone

*A range of measures will be needed to move forward, including ...*

To what extent might public policy tackle the main factors that are keeping children in poverty? Some important influences, such as the state of the economy, labour demand, characteristics of parents and patterns of family and household formation, are not directly controlled by governments. However, a number of policy levers can have a strong influence.

*... further cuts in worklessness, which will be constrained by the present profile of workless parents ...*

First, the present government has shown that employment policies can influence the number of children with parents in work. In particular, it has taken far more active measures to help and encourage lone parents to get jobs, whereas previously employment policy had been focused on those with an obligation to seek work as a condition of their benefits. Three main tools for doing so are improvement of work incentives through tax credits, the obligation to attend work-focused interviews and active assistance through the New Deal. Quantifying the contribution made by public policy is extremely difficult, but best estimates are that it has so far raised the proportion of couples with work by about 1 per cent and the proportion of lone parents with work by about 5 per cent[44].

Future gains of this kind will not be easy. As shown above, many claimants of benefits in workless households have characteristics that reduce the chance that they will get jobs, such as being disabled or having young children, and two thirds have been claiming benefits for at least two years. Nevertheless, it should be possible to continue to make progress, and several factors could combine to help the government to move towards its objective of raising lone-parent employment from 56 per cent to 70 per cent by 2010. Work carried out for this project[45] estimates that:

- existing welfare to work policies, including improvements in childcare and in work incentives, will add 4.5 percentage points to the lone-parent employment rate by 2010;
- policies already announced and funded will add a further half a percentage point;
- planned policies, particularly the expansion of Pathways and New Deal Plus for lone parents proposed in the Welfare Reform Green Paper could add 3.5-4.5 percentage points;
- these policy effects will come on top of an expected 3 percentage point rise in lone parents' employment as a result of the fact that their characteristics are changing: in particular they are becoming on average better educated and less likely to have very young children.

There are less obvious reasons to think that worklessness will fall among couples with children, who do not have a special New Deal directed at them, and many of whom have to deal simultaneously with their own disability or mental illness and with the responsibility of looking after children. The Pathways to Work programme should help some of those on disability benefits, but at best guess this will only reduce the worklessness rate among such families by about half a percentage point.

On the basis of these estimates, the percentage of lone parents in work would rise from 56 per cent to about 67.5 per cent by 2010, and the percentage of couples with children not working would fall from 5 per cent to 4.5 per cent.

In seeking further progress in these directions over the longer term, governments will need to keep their employment strategies under review and ask why in some cases they do not seem to be working as well as they should. For example, as discussed in the previous chapter, efforts to improve childcare do not yet seem to have removed this as a barrier to employment for many parents. More generally, strategies to improve labour force participation appear to have worked better in some parts of the country than in others. One place where they have worked less well is London. A review of evidence in the 2006 Budget[46] suggests that there is a considerable shortfall in lone parents' employment in London not explained by the characteristics of individuals. Factors such as shortage of affordable childcare and higher benefit withdrawal rates for people with high rents may contribute to this 'London effect'. This may require new kinds of strategy that are more region-specific in future versions of the New Deal.

*"Jobs are needed to help people find work! A lot of young people feel there is no hope, especially those at school 14-16 years old. In some areas of Merseyside teenagers have just given up – there is no work in their communities so what's the point? An example was given of a local department store advertising 15 vacancies and over 200 applicants." (small group session at Liverpool feedback event)*

*"There are lots of parents who want to work, but can they work? If parents in poverty have a sick child and they do not have an understanding school or friend who can help them out, then they have to pick up their child themselves. However, an employer would not let them do this or let them take a week off work without them having to go in and make the time up. The parents, children and families in poverty lose out." (parent at London feedback event)*

### ... further improvements in tax credits and benefits ...

Government fiscal policy has greatly favoured low-income families with children over recent years. On average, families with children in the poorest fifth of the population are £3,400 a year better off, in real terms, in 2006 than in 1997, as a result of changes in taxes and benefits plus the introduction of the National Minimum Wage[47]. Yet further changes in this direction are likely to be fundamental to any continued reduction in child poverty. The modelling in the following chapter focuses in particular on the cost and effects of further improvements in tax credits and benefits. In order to eradicate child poverty completely, these improvements will need to reach a range of people in different circumstances with low incomes, but policy design will need to pay particular attention to the situation of:

- people outside work, who have the deepest poverty and thus will need the greatest income rises to escape it;
- among working families, the situation of couples with children, who have been helped so far to a lesser extent by tax credits than lone parents, and now account for over 80 per cent of poor children in working families; and
- large families, who face a greater risk of poverty than small ones – for example, one poor child in five has at least three siblings, although only a tenth of all children do. This presents a case for at least considering large family supplements in the tax or benefit system.

*... and measures to help improve the pay and earnings of working parents.*
What levers does the government have to improve the amount gained from the market by poor families, which could play an important part in lifting them out of poverty? Such policies are more elusive, and harder to model, than straightforward redistribution. They include:

- Measures to improve education and skills, and hence productivity and wages. Over the long term, such policies could be fundamental in changing lifetime experiences in the labour market. There is also scope for more immediate help from the government in improving skills, and the Chancellor's aspiration to make the New Deal as much about gaining skills as about getting jobs, articulated in his 2006 Budget speech, points in that direction. Yet measures to raise the skills of disadvantaged groups in work remain underdeveloped.
- Other measures to improve pay. The National Minimum Wage has been seen as an obvious means to this end, but only affects people near the very bottom of the labour market. Perhaps just as important a tool would be equal pay for women, since the great majority of low-paid parents are mothers. The work of the Equalities Review is highlighting this issue, which will be an important part of the future anti-poverty agenda.
- Measures to improve the opportunity to increase the amount of work within a family. This includes lengthening the working hours of an individual and adding a second earner in a couple. Not all families would choose to extend their working hours, but for those that would choose to, new opportunities need to be made available. In particular, a neglected part of the 'welfare to work' agenda has been help and encouragement given to a non-working partner of someone already in work, if only to work part time. And promoting family-friendly policies that allow work and home commitments to be reconciled will be central to opening up more employment opportunities for parents.

*"Parents are constantly torn between whether they are going to do the right thing by their child or by their employer. Flexibility in employment would be really helpful for that. Working from home, flexible hours and all those things should be used, particularly for parents." (small group session at London feedback event)*

## Box 7: An agenda for tomorrow: thinking long term

The two most direct ways for governments to cut child poverty are to increase income transfers to poor families and to help parents into work. But in the long term these may not be the most important influences. The capacity of tomorrow's parents to lead fulfilling lives, free of poverty, will to a large extent be influenced by their early development, including their education. People with strong personal and vocational skills have greater control over their lives, with greater potential not just to hold down a job but also to achieve their desired balance between work and other aspects of life.

A big part of the unfinished agenda therefore concerns educational outcomes. The UK still has more children aged 17 outside education than other similar countries[48] and a steeper 'social gradient' dividing the knowledge and skills of students aged 15 according to socioeconomic background[49], while recent improvements in educational outcomes have still left one in four 19-year-olds without a basic qualification[50]. Tackling these inequalities by focusing on the needs of under-achievers and people from disadvantaged backgrounds will be crucial to tackling child poverty over the long term.

# 4 Modelling the future to 2020

*This chapter models solutions for meeting the government's child poverty targets ...*

The government's target is to cut child poverty to half its 1998/99 level by 2010 and to 'end' it by 2020. This chapter reports on the results of policy simulations co-ordinated by the Institute for Fiscal Studies (IFS), looking first at what the consequences of current policy are likely to be for child poverty and second what kinds of policies can be modelled that would enable the targets to be reached[51].

*... but can only take some factors into account, to demonstrate the scale of the task rather than give an exact prescription.*

The results presented in this chapter are based on micro-simulation modelling, which attempts to predict the distribution of household income – and therefore relative poverty – given forecasts of key demographic and economic trends, and details of future tax and benefit policies. The modelling was carried out by Mike Brewer and James Browne at the IFS, in partnership with Professor Holly Sutherland, and made use of demographic and economic forecasts provided by Professors Phil Rees and Paul Gregg.

This exercise is constrained by what it is possible to model: that is, where a particular policy has a reasonably predictable effect on household incomes. Some policies – such as improving education levels of tomorrow's parents – may be fundamental to the long-term reduction in child poverty, but their results cannot readily be projected. Although this chapter estimates the cost of only using tax credits, benefits and welfare to work policies to reduce child poverty, since these have a quantifiable impact, the report is not arguing that the government should rely exclusively on these policies.

Figure 9 shows which factors are inside and outside the model, and relates these to the wider picture of what kinds of trends will have an impact on child poverty. It starts by showing the context: a fairly even division between two groups facing poverty, the minority of children without workers in their households with a very high risk of being poor, and the much larger number of children in working families with a smaller risk of being poor. For the first group, most of the factors reducing poverty risk can be modelled because they depend on state transfers. For the second group, there are many more imponderables, since a number of factors can affect earnings, over which public policy only has limited influence. The third key issue is the relative size of the two groups – how many children have workers in their households. Public welfare to work measures affect this, and the model projects their impact based on certain assumptions. It also projects

## **Figure 9** Modelling reductions in child poverty

### a) Distribution of children in poverty (2004-05)

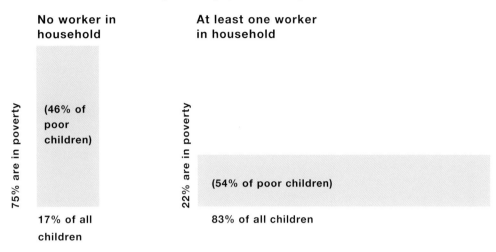

### b) How child poverty might come down, and what was modelled

Changes included in model shown in **CAPITALS**. Other factors were not explicitly modelled or assumed to have neutral effect.

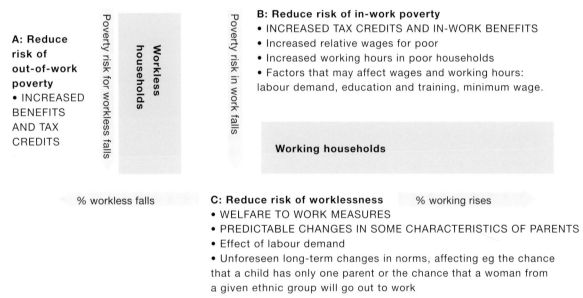

the effect of some predictable characteristics of parents, likely to affect poverty rates (see below). However, the impact of many other factors on the chances that parents will be in work remain highly unpredictable.

Thus, like any economic forecast, the results in this chapter are subject to considerable uncertainty whose importance is unknown, and these uncertainties are much greater for 2020 than for 2010. We do not attempt to predict the ups and downs of the economic cycle, or economic shocks, and so results must be understood as an illustration of what would happen 'on present trends', rather than a firm prediction of the future. Changes in the characteristics of the population are important for child poverty, and some key changes have been reflected in the forecasts. In general, their impact is favourable. Lone parents are becoming older and better qualified on average, which reduces their risk of worklessness and poverty. The ageing population is likely to slow growth overall in the long term, and this will make it relatively easier for poorer groups without market income to 'keep up' with rising living standards, and hence contain or reduce relative poverty.

Another thing to bear in mind is that the model presented in this chapter is 'static': it does not take account of the ways in which individuals move in and out of poverty, only giving snapshots of the characteristics of the whole population at given points of time. Ultimately, the goal should be to limit the damage caused by poverty during the course of people's lives, and to tackle the processes that create it. Thus the 'static' population profiles described by the model show only one part of the picture. Another is the extent to which individuals remain vulnerable to the recurrence of low income, for example if they are in insecure jobs or if their incomes have only been raised just above the poverty line.

## Box 8: Definition and measurement of child poverty targets

As in Chapters 1 to 3, poverty is here defined as being below 60 per cent median household income, so for poverty to fall, poorer groups' incomes must not just rise in real terms, but must rise faster than the median. However, the formula for adjusting household income according to family composition ('equivalisation') is different in this (future-oriented) chapter than in the previous ones, because from 2007, the government will be adopting a new, internationally standardised definition. (This is the OECD scale rather than the 'McClements scale' hitherto used in the UK.) For child poverty, this uses a *before* housing costs measure, which was 26 per cent in 1998/99 with a target for 2010 of 13 per cent, rather than 33 per cent and 16.5 per cent respectively for the *after* housing costs measure reported above. The choice of measure makes little difference to the *number* of children taken out of poverty by any particular policy. However, because more children are in poverty before than after housing costs, the choice of a before housing cost measure produces higher *percentage* reductions than if an after housing cost measure were used, and therefore makes it easier to reach the targets, expressed as percentage reductions.

Various interpretations have been put on what it means to 'end' child poverty. Getting the numbers all the way to zero is generally seen as unrealistic: in a 'snapshot' survey, some people always have very low or even negative incomes, which can for example be caused by a temporary business loss. Here we have used the ambitious criterion of getting child poverty below about 5 per cent, which is around the lowest ever achieved in any European country. This would be a cut by over 80 per cent in the number of children in poverty compared to 1998/99.

## The 'steady as she goes' scenario

What would happen to child poverty in 2010 and 2020 if present policies were continued? These policies include:

- The measures mentioned in Chapter 3 to improve employment.
- The pledge, so far to the end of the present Parliament, to increase the child element of Child Tax Credit (that is, the portion targeted on low-income children) in line with earnings. We assume here that this policy is continued, which would require £1.8 billion more to be spent per year in 2020 than currently budgeted for.
- The uprating of most out-of-work benefits, of Child Benefit and of the Working Tax Credit in line with prices.
- The freezing of the family element of the Child Tax Credit.

*Present policies will contain child poverty but not reduce it.*
The consequences of these policies are shown in Figure 10. The results show clearly that even if current policies succeed in expanding employment as well as putting more in real terms into the Child Tax Credit, child poverty will not continue on its steady downward trend of the past few years. There will be a small numerical fall in the number of children in poverty, but this will fall far short of meeting government targets. Indeed, by 2010 the

## Figure 10 Child poverty with existing policies

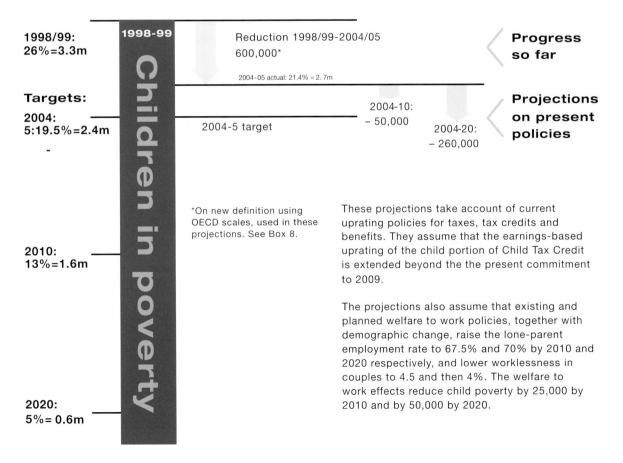

1998/99:
26%=3.3m

**Progress so far**

1998-99

Reduction 1998/99-2004/05
600,000*

2004-05 actual: 21.4% = 2.7m

Targets:

2004:
5:19.5%=2.4m

2004-5 target

2004-10:
– 50,000

2004-20:
– 260,000

**Projections on present policies**

*On new definition using OECD scales, used in these projections. See Box 8.

These projections take account of current uprating policies for taxes, tax credits and benefits. They assume that the earnings-based uprating of the child portion of Child Tax Credit is extended beyond the the present commitment to 2009.

2010:
13%=1.6m

The projections also assume that existing and planned welfare to work policies, together with demographic change, raise the lone-parent employment rate to 67.5% and 70% by 2010 and 2020 respectively, and lower worklessness in couples to 4.5 and then 4%. The welfare to work effects reduce child poverty by 25,000 by 2010 and by 50,000 by 2020.

2020:
5%= 0.6m

Children in poverty

percentage of children in poverty will be slightly higher than in 2004-05, but with a small fall in the child population, the absolute number in poverty will be about 2 per cent lower. This compares to a 41 per cent fall needed to reach the target. By 2020 child poverty will have fallen by 8 per cent, compared to the 78 per cent fall needed.

Thus, tax and benefit policies combined with welfare to work are only just enough to prevent poverty from rising again, and not nearly enough to cut it by around a million by 2010 and a further million by 2020. To maintain and increase the momentum of recent falls in child poverty, more is needed.

## Box 9: Percentage-based targets and the number of children in poverty

The child poverty targets have been interpreted in terms of the reduction of the *percentage* of children in poverty. With a falling child population, this means that the *number* of poor children has to fall, for example, by slightly more than 50 per cent by 2010 in order for the percentage to halve. For presentational purposes, the following discussion and graphs are expressed mainly in terms of the number of children in poverty. The targets, however, are based on percentages in poverty, multiplied by the child population in the relevant year.

The reason for the lack of further progress, on current policies only, is clear. With incomes overall growing steadily, the family incomes of poor children have to grow substantially faster in order to cross the relative poverty line. Some will do so by moving into work, but as explained in Chapter 3, in future this is unlikely to make more than a small contribution relative to the targets. The commitment to raise the per-child element of the Child Tax Credit, which goes to low-income families, in line with earnings, will stabilise rather than raise this portion of family income in relative terms. But if other parts of their income fall in relative terms, poverty could deepen. This remains a risk for all families, since Child Benefit is uprated relative to prices rather than earnings, but most particularly for out-of-work families who depend heavily on Income Support, which also rises with prices.

## The cost-effectiveness of three individual policies to 2010

*Increases in taxes or benefits can reduce poverty effectively, but only using Child Benefit is not cost-efficient.*

Over the long term, a variety of policies that improve employment as well as pay prospects for parents, together with a gradual improvement in the generosity of tax credits and benefits, could continue to make inroads into child poverty. However, in order to get back on track to meet the 2010 targets, more immediate and drastic measures would be needed, transferring more resources to families with low incomes. Figure 11 shows the cost-effectiveness of three alternative policies seeking to reduce poverty to below half its 1998/99 level by the end of this decade.

## Figure 11 Projected fall in child poverty 2004-10

(i) with individual policies

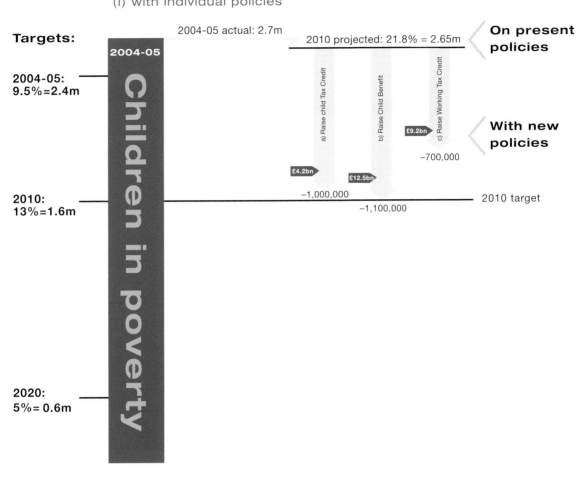

### The cost-effectiveness of these three policies for reducing child poverty by 2010

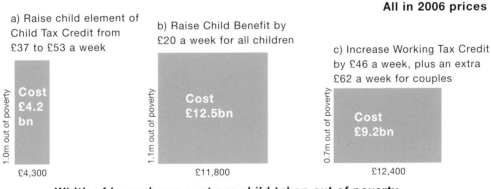

**Width of bars shows cost per child taken out of poverty**

The most cost-effective single mechanism to reduce child poverty is raising the child element of the Child Tax Credit, which is targeted at low-income families both inside and outside work. This payment is presently £37 a week per child and rising with earnings. Increasing it much faster than earnings – by almost half in real terms by 2010 – would cost £4.2 billion, and would bring child poverty almost to the 13 per cent target. On the other hand, to meet the target using Child Benefit, paid at the same rate to all families regardless of income, would cost three times as much. A third mechanism that would contribute to a decline in poverty is raising the Working Tax Credit. If this went up steeply for all parents, and the rate for couples were raised to reflect the greater needs of two adults rather than one[52] (which does not happen today), some progress could be made in bringing poverty down. However, it is expensive to do this using Working Tax Credit on its own, and half of children in poverty – those without working parents – would remain unaffected by this change. In the illustration, therefore, this policy does not succeed in hitting the 2010 target.

## Policy packages for 2010

In practice, any one of these policies is likely to seem unbalanced. Putting too much emphasis on one measure can create distortions. For example, the most cost-effective single measure, raising the targeted portion of the Child Tax Credit, could have work incentive implications by bringing many more working families into a means-tested tax credit system with sharp withdrawal rates as income rises. Is it possible instead to find a cost-effective package using several policies?

Figuro 12 shows three possible combinations of policies with similar costs, each of which would meet the 2010 target. The cost of each combination of policies is also similar to the lowest-cost single measure discussed above, the rise in the child element of Child Tax Credit. Although they involve rises that are less narrowly means tested than relying on that element alone, a different form of targeting – by size of family – helps to ensure a reasonable amount of the new money finds its way to children in poverty.

*One option is to use all three of the above measures ...*
Package A suggests rises in all three of the tax credits/benefits mentioned above. Both the child element of Child Tax Credit and Child Benefit for the third and subsequent children would rise faster than earnings (although not as fast as in the previous, single-policy illustrations), and a one-off increase in Working Tax Credit for couples would give extra resources to provide for a second adult, as discussed previously.

*... but extending the 'progressive universalism' of the Child Tax Credit looks promising ...*
Package B would involve rises only in the Child Tax Credit, but would use its two elements for two different purposes. The child element would, as in Package A, help low-income families more by rising relative to earnings. But a greater rise would be given to children in large families, by increasing the 'family element' of the credit by £20 a week for the third and for each subsequent child. This element goes to nearly 90 per cent of families with children, so larger families with all but the highest incomes would gain. This would help maintain the principle of 'progressive universalism', which gives a certain level of benefits to people with particular needs regardless of their incomes, but more for the least well-off. The targeting of large families regardless of income as well as poor families in this package has advantages. It reduces work disincentives, and increases the degree

**Figure 12** Projected fall in child poverty 2004-10

(ii) with policy packages

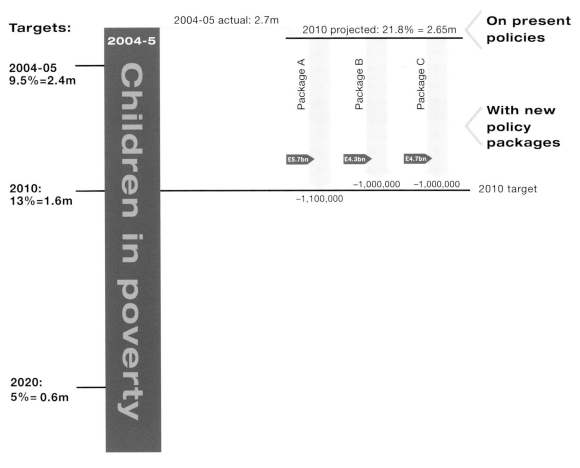

**The cost-effectiveness of these three policies
for reducing child poverty by 2010**

All in 2006 prices

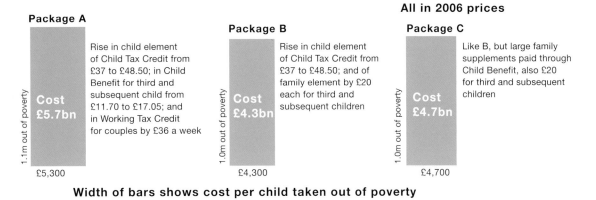

Width of bars shows cost per child taken out of poverty

to which large families can rely on a certain level of child support that will not fluctuate with their incomes. Moreover, because of the relatively high poverty rates experienced by larger families, it is just as cost-efficient as using the child portion of Child Tax Credit only in lifting children out of poverty.

*... although another option would be to focus more on Child Benefit.*

Package C is similar to Package B, but uses Child Benefit rather than the Child Tax Credit to give more to larger families. This involves a very large rise in Child Benefit for the third and subsequent children: it would rise from £11.70 now to £35.74 in 2010, rather than to £13.05 if it only rose in line with prices. Although this is not much more expensive than Package B, it seems unlikely that such a large increase would appear just, especially since it would go to all families with large numbers of children, including richer ones. However, this option illustrates how at least some of the task of reducing poverty could be achieved by raising Child Benefit for larger families, without adding substantially to the cost of poverty reduction.

*These 2010 options are expensive but affordable.*

The extra cost of these strategies for halving poverty by 2010, around £4 to £5 billion in today's money, is considerable but not unaffordable, if the country puts a priority on keeping this historic mission on track. In 2006 prices £4.5 billion is equivalent to about 0.3 per cent of GDP in 2010. The UK economy grows by this amount, in real terms, every month and a half. Moreover, this extra £4 to £5 billion is relative to current policy, which is based on only uprating most benefits and tax credits with prices, and therefore on redistributing a declining share of a growing national cake to people on low incomes. Hitting the poverty target in 2010 would cost about £1.7 billion more than the cost of uprating all benefits and tax credits for parents in line with earnings growth. It therefore only represents a very small increase in the share of national income devoted to supporting the income of families with children.

**Policy packages for 2020**

*Between 2010 and 2020, progress will require even more vigorous efforts ...*

Achieving the target of taking all or nearly all remaining children out of poverty by 2020 will be a much harder task. The modelling work found that simply increasing benefits and tax credits brings diminishing returns in reducing poverty as it falls further, to the extent that by the time child poverty approaches 5 per cent, it costs tens or even hundreds of thousands of pounds in extra spending to take each extra child out of poverty. This is partly because tax credits fail to reach some families, who do not claim them. If take-up rates rise, on the other hand, it is possible to increase tax credits and benefits to the point where child poverty falls below 5 per cent, at a high but not absurd cost. Therefore, in suggesting packages for 2010-20, the modelling has assumed that the government adopts measures to improve take-up, and succeeds in reducing non-take-up of tax credits by half during this period.

Two packages for reducing poverty between 2010 and 2020 are illustrated in Figure 13. These packages assume as a starting point that Package B, the lowest cost option for reaching the 2010 target, has been implemented, and then existing policies are carried forward for the next decade. This would include earnings uprating not just for the income-targeted child element of Child Tax Credit as now, but also for the new supplement

# Figure 13: Projected fall in child poverty 2010–20

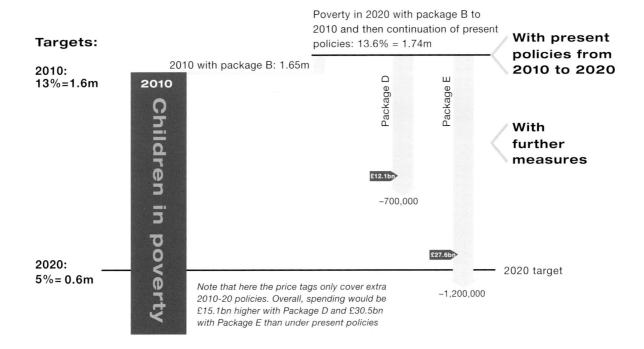

**Targets:**

**2010:**
**13%=1.6m**

**2020:**
**5%= 0.6m**

Poverty in 2020 with package B to 2010 and then continuation of present policies: 13.6% = 1.74m

2010 with package B: 1.65m

2010

Children in poverty

Package D

Package E

**With present policies from 2010 to 2020**

**With further measures**

£12.1bn

−700,000

£27.6bn

2020 target

−1,200,000

*Note that here the price tags only cover extra 2010-20 policies. Overall, spending would be £15.1bn higher with Package D and £30.5bn with Package E than under present policies*

**The cost-effectiveness of these two policies for reducing child poverty by 2020**

**All in 2006 prices**

**Package D: Extend indexation**
Uprates with earnings all benefits and tax credits for parents from 2010, and raises Working Tax Credit for couples*

0.7m out of poverty

Cost
£12.1bn

£16,900

**Package E: Spend what it takes**
Additionally uprates key parts of parents' incomes 5% a year faster than earnings: child element of Child Tax Credit, Income Support, Housing Benefit disregards*

1.2m out of poverty

Cost
£27.6bn

£22,600

**Width of bars shows cost per child taken out of poverty**

*\* Both of these packages also assume that the government makes extra efforts to improve tax credit take-up, and by 2020 succeeds in halving the present rate of non-take-up. Without this assumption, spending on tax and benefits yield sharply diminishing returns, and it is virtually impossible to reach the target poverty level.*

targeted at large families. However, simply continuing these policies would not only fail to achieve any further reductions in child poverty but would lead to a small rise – by about 90,000, to 1,740,000 children. As at present, keeping part of children's income in line with earnings is not enough to stem a rise in relative poverty if other parts are falling behind. This effect would be all the more important once poverty had been halved by 2010, as this would bring some non-working families just above the poverty line, increasing the number who might fall below it if the relative value of Income Support continues to fall. (It also demonstrates how 'lifting a child out of poverty' is not a permanent achievement, and if they remain close to the poverty line, they remain vulnerable over time.) Another reason why progress is difficult after 2010 is that credible assumptions about employment entail a slowing down in the reduction in worklessness, given that such a large proportion of the remaining workless households are either disabled or are lone parents with young children (see Chapter 3).

### ... and would require benefits to be uprated at least as fast as earnings ...

Against this background, it would be ineffective to rely only on tax credits and benefits specifically directed at the needs of children to reduce child poverty to the 2020 level. For example, even if Child Tax Credit were *doubled* relative to earnings, at a cost of £20 billion, child poverty in 2020 would still be nearly 9 per cent, compared to the 5 per cent target. Some progress is also needed in maintaining or raising the relative value of the rest of parents' incomes. A mixed package involving the uprating of all the main benefits and tax credits going to families with children, at least in line with earnings would provide a more balanced and (relatively) more cost-effective means of reducing poverty.

### ... with much greater rises needed to get close to the 2020 target ...

A first step in the right direction (Package D) could be taken by increasing in line with earnings all tax credits and benefits for families with children, as well as uprating Working Tax Credit for couples as discussed above. This would get child poverty down to 8.4 per cent – lower than at any time in Britain since relevant data became available in 1960. But to get below the 5 per cent target would also require key benefits and tax credits to rise much faster than earnings, an extremely costly policy, illustrated in Package E. (If there were full tax credit take-up, rather than a halving of non-take-up as assumed here, child poverty under this package would fall below 3 per cent.) The marginal cost of getting each of these last 500,000 children out of poverty[53] would be nearly twice as high as for the previous 700,000, which in turn costs nearly four times as much per child as for the previous million, taken out before 2010.

Note that the final option would involve roughly a doubling in real terms of the relevant benefits and tax credits between 2010 and 2020. This would make payments to poor families with children look very generous indeed, especially in contrast to benefits for those without children that had been going up only with inflation. For example, a single woman on Jobseeker's Allowance would receive £55 a week, but if she had a baby and became a lone parent, her income would rise to nearly £200 (not including the temporary baby premium) in 2006 prices.

### ... and although we can afford the cost if we want to ...

Even the very high costs of these measures need to be put in perspective. Package D would require us to spend 0.7 per cent more of our GDP in 2020 on tackling poverty than without this package, and Package E would require us to spend 1.6 per cent more. In the whole 14-year period between now and 2020, this would increase spending by 1.8 per cent of GDP compared to current policies extended over that period. The bill is in fact 1.9 per cent of GDP higher than spending under current commitments, which only promise to continue uprating the child element of Child Tax Credit with earnings during the current Parliament. Spending this extra 1.9 per cent of GDP would make the difference between reducing child poverty to under 5 per cent and seeing it start to rise again.

These extra costs would have to be incurred by an economy that tends to grow by about 2.5 per cent a year in real terms. So solving the problem primarily through fiscal means would pre-empt less than one year's worth of the economic growth expected over the next 14 years. This would, it is true, require an increase in the proportion of income raised in taxation. However, one aspect of current budgetary practice, as opposed to Treasury budget projections, would yield most of the cost of these measures through higher taxes. Uprating tax allowances only with prices rather than earnings gradually increases the proportion of income raised in tax, yet the long-term Treasury forecasts assume that they will be indexed to earnings. For this reason, if current budgetary practice is followed, tax revenues will by 2020 be £23 billion more (in 2006 prices) than is currently assumed.

*... a more plausible scenario combines redistribution with improved market incomes.*

Nevertheless, the escalating marginal cost of getting children out of poverty through tax and benefit policy in the 2010-20 scenarios is an important signal of the need for a multifaceted strategy that benefits from but does not rely solely on these measures. A key long-term requirement is to increase substantially the amount that parents earn from work. This would have the double advantage of lifting more families out of poverty with the help of market incomes and reducing the cost of the tax credit system and so releasing resources to raise benefits for those remaining out of work. It is interesting to note that even as the poverty rate falls below 10 per cent in the model discussed here, a third of poor children still live in single-earner couples. Helping such families to do better in the labour market is an important part of the overall equation.

*In considering the above models, some account must be taken of work incentives ...*

To interpret the above modelling results, some further considerations need to be taken into account. The first is that the projected movements in benefits and tax credits could have some consequences on work incentives and hence on behaviour, with potential knock-on effects. In most cases the results above do not take account of such behavioural changes, although for the 2010 policy illustration of raising the Working Tax Credit, a positive effect on employment has been assumed. However, the effect of raising the Child Tax Credit by the large amounts suggested in the packages would be to give means-tested tax credits to more families, and these families would face high marginal withdrawal rates as their income rose. This could in particular deter couples from having second earners, and the estimated effect would be to reduce by 90,000 the number of couples where a second person works. This would not have a drastic feedback effect on poverty (many of those affected would have been taken out of poverty by the higher tax credits), although it could deter a number of families from improving their living standards further.

*... and of the sensitivity of the model to various uncertainties.*

A further consideration in interpreting the model is the extent to which its results would be different if some of the assumptions built into it turned out to be wrong. Higher rents and council taxes would reduce relative poverty, since people receiving benefit support to help pay for these items are better protected from the effects than the median household against which their incomes are being compared. Similarly, if real earnings grow more slowly, relative poverty tends to fall since many benefits rise at a given rate regardless of what happens to earnings. A failure of the demographic changes forecast by the model to materialise might cause poverty to be higher than expected. While all these variations would have an effect, the impact is not dramatic. Within plausible variations, the effect of any one factor is generally less than one percentage point in the poverty rate under policy scenarios to 2020. Thus, the model gives a good general idea of the impact of the policies under review.

# 5 Conclusion
## Firing on all cylinders

With determination, child poverty can be consigned to the UK's history books. Yet there is no single measure that will make it possible to do so. Rather, a strategy to end child poverty requires a range of measures to distribute resources to low-income families, to improve individual opportunities and to build a society in which rewards are more evenly distributed and in which everyone gets a chance to participate fully.

This report has demonstrated that the gains of the past decade, which have owed much to rising employment levels and to redistribution through tax credits, cannot be sustained simply by continuing present policies. Further employment gains will help bring some children out of poverty, but nowhere near enough to meet targets. Rises in tax credits and benefits for families with children, on present uprating policies, combined with welfare to work policies, will only be enough to prevent child poverty rising, not to make it fall further.

A further jump in the generosity of tax credits, by about half as much as the big rise in Labour's first two terms, could allow the 2010 target to be met. Between 1998 and 2003, the government announced changes to benefits and tax credits for children that increased spending in this area by 0.7 per cent of GDP; by 2010 the government needs to announce changes worth a further 0.3 per cent for child poverty to have been halved in just over a decade. However, in getting the second half of children out of poverty to meet the 2020 target, a tax credit-led strategy becomes increasingly costly, requiring a further 1.6 per cent of GDP. Under these scenarios, while from 1998 to 2010, 1.7 million children would have escaped poverty through increased spending of 1 per cent of GDP, from 2010 to 2020 it would be a 1.2 million fall for 1.6 per cent of GDP – over twice the cost pro rata.

Moreover, relying mainly on tax credit and benefit rises to meet the 2020 target would require such large rises in entitlements that the system may seem distorted and ultimately unjust. Large financial 'rewards' to people on low incomes for having children and even larger ones for having three or more, while targeting child poverty, could be seen as an undue encouragement for people to have children without having the means to support them.

The conclusion must be that only a more balanced, wider range of measures can succeed. Welfare to work and tax credits provide the first main two prongs of the government's anti-poverty strategy. Two more prongs in particular will be essential. One is still about redistribution: the raising of the relative value of the incomes of non-working families, by increasing the 'adult' portion (principally Income Support) as well as the 'child' portion (principally Child Tax Credit) of these incomes. Given that significant numbers of families will remain outside work at any one time, child poverty cannot be reduced to negligible levels until out-of-work incomes rise above the poverty line.

The second new prong is to improve earnings from work among the poorest working families. This is a wide agenda. It will be influenced less by direct government decisions such as the level of the Minimum Wage, than by long-term developments in labour markets and in skills. In particular, a successful education policy today would ensure that more parents in 2020 are able to earn enough to keep their families out of poverty without massive help through tax credits.

These two new prongs, which would help raise incomes inside and outside work, are in fact complementary. Higher earned incomes would help not only to get families out of poverty but also release money from tax credits topping up low earnings. This money could help pay for higher benefits, offsetting the high cost of increasing Income Support. This point was driven home in the modelling work, where assumptions about more people moving into work did not, under present wage and tax credit patterns, lead to much of a financial saving. For some groups, we are spending almost as much topping up low wages as we would paying out-of-work benefits. Until market incomes make a greater contribution, the public cost of ending child poverty will be very great indeed.

Thus, ending child poverty means firing on all cylinders. Substantially greater payments to families than currently envisaged will be a necessary but not a sufficient condition for meeting the targets, especially not the longer-term target set for 2020.

We therefore need to think about two big issues for carrying these ambitions forward. First, we need to think harder about where money will come from to continue improving redistribution to lower-income families. More taxes will be needed from somewhere. Until now, higher taxes have to a large extent been engineered through 'fiscal drag' – the failure to uprate tax thresholds as incomes rise, and therefore the collection of a larger fraction of national income in tax. A continuation of this policy would go a long way towards raising resources needed to end child poverty, if all the gains were allocated to this purpose, but other public spending claims will compete for this money. A debate about ending child poverty therefore also requires a debate about taxation.

The second big issue is how to think in the long term not just about 'how we help the poor' but also about 'how we avert poverty'. At the heart of this issue is education. Today's schoolchildren are tomorrow's parents. If they leave school with more transferable skills that make them employable, more will enter jobs and more will be able to earn a decent living when they do work. Improved investment in the education of disadvantaged children is a policy whose effects cannot be accurately modelled, but one that nevertheless must be at the heart of a long-term anti-poverty strategy.

# Notes

1 David Gordon et al (2000) *Poverty and social exclusion in Britain*, York: Joseph Rowntree Foundation.

2 See, for example, David Piachaud (2005) 'Child poverty, an overview', in Gabriel Preston (ed) *At greatest risk*, London: CPAG.

3 Nick Lyon, Matt Barnes and Daniel Sweiry (2006) *Families with children in Britain: Findings from the 2004 Families and Children Study* (FACS), DWP Research Report No 340, London: DWP, p 201.

4 This assumes nobody other than parent(s) and their dependent children lives in the household. Where people outside this nuclear family share the household it becomes more complex, since poverty is measured through household rather than family income.

5 See, for example, David Darton, Donald Hirsch and Jason Strelitz (2003) *Tackling disadvantage, A 20-year enterprise*, York: Joseph Rowntree Foundation, p 14.

6 The four examples given here are some of the groups identified in Gabriel Preston (ed) (2005) *At greatest risk*, London: CPAG. Among various other groups at high risk are children of problem drug users and children with a parent in prison.

7 For a review of their situation see Sue Regan (2005) 'Children in acute housing need, in Gabriel Preston (ed) *At greatest risk*, London: CPAG.

8 Hugh Stickland and Richard Olsen (2005) 'Children with disabled parents', in Gabriel Preston (ed) *At greatest risk*, London: CPAG.

9 Pamela Fitzpatrick (2005) 'Asylum seeker families', in Gabriel Preston (ed) *At greatest risk*, London: CPAG.

10 See Sarah Cemlyn and Colin Clark, (2005) 'The social exclusion of Gypsy and Traveller children', in Gabriel Preston (ed) *At greatest risk*, London: CPAG.

11 See Donald Hirsch (2004) *Strategies against poverty – A shared road map*, York: Joseph Rowntree Foundation.

12 At present, different surveys come to contradictory conclusions. Paddy Hillyard, Grace Kelly, Eithne McLaughlin, Demi Patsios and Mike Tomlinson (2003) *Bare necessities – Poverty and social exclusion in Northern Ireland: key findings*, Belfast: Democratic Dialogue, appears to show that child poverty in Northern Ireland is substantially higher than in Britain. Department for Work and Pensions (2006) *Households below average income 1994/5-2004-5*, London: The Stationery Office, seems to show that the rates are around the same before housing costs, and lower in Northern Ireland than Britain when measured after housing costs. Flaws in data sampling may help explain this difference, but the reason needs to be probed further.

13 Goretti Horgan (2005) 'Child Poverty in Northern Ireland: the Limits of welfare-to-work policies', *Social Policy and Administration*, vol 39 no 1, February, pp49-64.

14 Commission on Families and the Wellbeing of Children (2005) *Families and the state – Two-way support and responsibilities*, Bristol: The Policy Press, p 60, citing especially J Corlyon, S Hunter and I Katz (2006: forthcoming) *The relationship between parenting and poverty*, York: Joseph Rowntree Foundation.

15 See Donald Hirsch (2006) *The cost of not ending child poverty – How we can think about it, how it might be measured, and some evidence*, Working paper (www.jrf.org.uk/child-poverty).

16 Barnardo's (2000) *Counting the cost of child poverty,* London: Barnardo's.

17 Jo Blanden and Steve Gibbons (2006) *The persistence of poverty across generations: A view from two British cohorts*, Bristol: The Policy Press.

18 European Community Household Panel survey, Eurostat.

19 Luxembourg Income Study.

20 Guy Palmer et al (2005) *Monitoring poverty and social exclusion 2005*, York: Joseph Rowntree Foundation, p 41.

21 *OECD Employment Outlook 2001*, p 134, shows the UK as the country where the highest proportion of parents in the Organisation for Economic Co-operation and Development (OECD) are lone parents. In most countries, over 60 per cent of lone parents worked, compared to around 40 per cent in the UK at the time of the survey in 1999, and just over 50 per cent by 2005.

22 Stephen Machin (2003) 'Wage inequality since 1975', in Richard Dickens et al (eds) *The Labour market under new Labour*, Basingstoke: Palgrave, p 195.

23 Jane Millar and Karen Gardiner (2004) *Low pay, household resources and poverty*, York: Joseph Rowntree Foundation, p 22. Low pay is defined here as below two thirds median pay.

24 That is, two parents working full time or a lone parent working full time.

25 Monica Magadi and Sue Middleton (2005) *Britain's poorest children revisited: Evidence from the BHPS (1994-2002)*, London: Save the Children, pp 116-17.

26 Paul Gregg, Susan Harkness and Lindsey Macmillian, (2006) *A review of issues relating to the labour market and economy, particularly in terms of the impact of labour market initiatives on children's income poverty*, Working paper (www.jrf.org.uk/child-poverty).

27 Nick Gould (2006) *Mental health and child poverty*, Working paper (www.jrf.org.uk/child-poverty).

28 Summarised in Stephen Machin and Sandra McNally (2006) *Education and child poverty: Literature review*, Working paper (www.jrf.org.uk/child-poverty).

29 Steve McIntosh and Anna Vignoles (2000) *Measuring and assessing the impact of basic skills on labour market outcomes*, CEE Discussion Paper No 3, London: London School of Economics Centre for the Economics of Education.

30 Stephen Machin and Sandra McNally (2006) *Education and child poverty: Literature review*, Working paper (www.jrf.org.uk/child-poverty).

31 Christine Skinner (2006) *Childcare: A review of the evidence*, Working paper (www.jrf.org.uk/child-poverty).

32 Jane Millar and Karen Gardiner (2004) *Low pay, household resources and poverty*, York: Joseph Rowntree Foundation, p 37. The other sources of income are largely from others in the household, such as grown-up children.

33 Ibid.

34 In 2004/05, a low-income family was entitled to an extra £42.30 in Child Tax Credit and Child Benefit for each child after the first one. The adjustment in income needs

used in equivalising income of someone close to the poverty line would have been by less than this amount for additional children up to age 10, but by more for older children – for example, £51 for a 13-year-old (see Box 1 above).

35 See Jonathan Bradshaw, Naomi Finch, Ernese Mayhew, Veli-Matti Ritakallio and Christine Skinner (2006) *Child poverty in large families*, Bristol: The Policy Press/JRF.

36 Jonathan Bradshaw (2006) *How has the child poverty rate and composition changed?*, Working paper (www.jrf.org.uk/child-poverty).

37 Mike Brewer, Alissa Goodman, Jonathan Shaw and Luke Sibieta (2006), *Poverty and inequality in Britain 2006,* London: Institute for Fiscal Studies.

38 For example, Stephen Machin (2003) 'Wage inequality since 1975', in Richard Dickens, Paul Gregg and Jonathan Wadsworth, *The labour market under new Labour*, Basingstoke: Palgrave Macmillan shows that relative wages have stabilised in recent years, following widening inequality in previous decades.

39 Brewer et al, op cit.

40 Paul Gregg, Susan Harkness and Lindsey Macmillan (2006) *A review of issues relating to the labour market and economy, particularly in terms of the impact of labour market initiatives on children's income poverty*, Working paper (www.jrf.org.uk/child-poverty).

41 Brewer et al, op cit.

42 Figures for August 2005, Department for Work and Pensions' Tabulation Tool.

43 Millar and Gardiner, op cit.

44 Paul Gregg, Susan Harkness and Lindsey Macmillan (2006) *A review of issues relating to the labour market and economy, particularly in terms of the impact of labour market initiatives on children's income poverty*, Working paper (www.jrf.org.uk/child-poverty).

45 Ibid.

46 HM Treasury (2006) *Employment opportunity for all: Examining labour market trends in London*, London: HM Treasury.

47 2006 HM Treasury Budget, p 101.

48 OECD (2004) *Education at a glance 2004*, Paris: OECD, p 279.

49 OECD (2001) *Knowledge and skills for life, First results from PISA 2000*, Paris: OECD, p 308.

50 Guy Palmer, Jane Carr and Peter Kenway (2005) *Monitoring poverty and social exclusion 2005*, York: Joseph Rowntree Foundation.

51 For a full description of this modelling and its results, see *Micro-simulating child poverty in 2010 and 2020* by Mike Brewer, James Browne and Holly Sutherland, JRF Working Paper (www.jrf.org.uk).

52 The basis for this rise, here and in Packages A, D and E below, assumes that the relative amounts paid to meet the needs of a couple compared to a lone parent should be the same in Working Tax Credit as it is in Income Support. This implies that the couple element of Working Tax Credit should be 57 per cent higher than the lone-parent element, rather than identical as it is today.

53 That is, the extra cost of adopting Package E rather than Package D, divided by the extra children brought out of poverty by doing so.

# Appendix
## Inputs to this report

This report draws on a range of published sources. These include a number of working papers commissioned for this project, all of which can be downloaded from the JRF website (www.jrf.org.uk/child-poverty/).

| | |
|---|---|
| Education and child poverty: literature review | Stephen Machin and Sandra McNally |
| Mental health and child poverty | Nick Gould |
| A review of the comparative evidence on child poverty | Jonathan Bradshaw |
| The cost of not ending child poverty – how we can think about it, how it might be measured, and some evidence | Donald Hirsch |
| Childcare | Christine Skinner |
| Welfare to work policies and child poverty: A review of issues relating to the labour market and economy | Paul Gregg, Susan Harkness and Lindsey Macmillan |
| Child support | Jonathan Bradshaw |
| Teenage births | Jonathan Bradshaw |
| How has the child poverty rate and composition changed? | Jonathan Bradshaw |
| Socio-demographic scenarios for children to 2020 | Philip Rees and John Parsons |
| Micro-simulating child poverty in 2010 and 2020 | Mike Brewer, James Browne and Holly Sutherland |

## Feedback events

Six feedback events were held between February and April 2006 in London, Sheffield, Liverpool, Glasgow, Belfast and Cardiff. Between 15 and 70 people took part in each event. These included families living on a low income, local service providers and charities and voluntary groups. The events were organised by the End Child Poverty Coalition in partnership with the following organisations:

- Northern Ireland Anti-Poverty Network
- Church Action on Poverty
- OFFER (Sheffield's Community Empowerment Network)
- Voluntary Action Sheffield
- The Out of School Network
- Sharrow Citizens' Advice Bureau
- End Child Poverty Cymru
- ATD Fourth World
- The Poverty Alliance
- The People's Centre
- UK Coalition Against Poverty
- Merseyside Network for Europe

The findings of the feedback events were fed into this report. A fuller report of the views expressed at the events will be published separately, in partnership with the End Child Poverty coalition (www.ecpc.org.uk).